D0330871

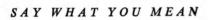

SAY WHAT YOU MEAN

RUDOLF FLESCH

Say What You Mean

HARPER & ROW, PUBLISHERS, INC.

New York, Evanston, San Francisco, London

1817

STANDARD BOOK NUMBER: 06–011291–3

LIBRARY OF CONGRESS CATALOG CARD NUMBER: 72–79664

Designed by Sidney Feinberg

Again, to Elizabeth

Contents

SAY WHAT YOU MEAN

1 *Learn to Write—Again*

"Have you ever done any writing?"

For some thirty years I've asked this question of every new student in my training classes for employees, civil servants, lawyers, doctors, engineers, bankers. Almost all of them said no. "Except on the job, of course," they'd say. "And papers in school . . . in college . . . in law school . . . but otherwise, no."

"Did you write for the school paper?" I'd insist.

Again the answer was no.

"Did you do any extracurricular writing at all? Send things to magazines and get rejection slips?"

No, no, nothing of the sort.

Only very, very few of all the students I've taught had ever felt an itch to write. The rest—99 percent or more—were born non-writers and stayed that way all their lives. For them, writing had always been an unpleasant chore; answering a simple letter loomed ahead as something like a visit to the dentist.

It seems that this is the common condition of mankind. I don't expect you to be different. Most probably the job of studying this book and learning how to improve your writing fills you with dismay. You're *not* looking forward to it. But you have to do a certain amount of writing in your job or career and you know that your writing is poor.

So you've decided to do something about it and tackle once more grammar, rhetoric, composition and good usage—all those dull, boring matters you learned year after year in school and have long since forgotten.

Knowing how you feel, I'll keep these dry, elementary matters to a minimum. Most likely, these things are not your problem anyway. You *don't* need more grammar, punctuation and usage. You probably have a pretty good grip on these essentials and only occasionally need to look up a point of spelling or style. What you really need is instruction in the basic principles of professional writing.

Why professional writing? you say. You don't want to be a writer; you're not interested in writing the Great American Novel or even in adding to your income with an occasional story or article. I know. But as a writer of business letters, memos, reports and other pieces of paper with words on them, you ought to know how writing is done by those who do it for a living. Only if you learn how to use professional techniques will you be able to improve the writing you have to do for your own purposes.

This will mean a basic change in your attitude. Right now, whenever you sit down to write or dictate a letter or report, you simply do it the way you've always done it, continuing habits that go back to your early school days and unconsciously trying to please an elementary school teacher or get high marks on a test. You're not really writing a letter to the addressee in the upper-left-hand corner or a report for your vice-president. Rather, you're writing a composition by the rules of the "English composition" game you were taught to play in school.

The first thing you have to learn is that this game isn't played in real life. There the rules are different. The pros—the novelists, magazine writers, newspapermen—have learned long ago that they must use "spoken" English and must avoid "written" English like the plague. The kind of writing you do every day—and receive every day in your incoming mail—may be flawless as a school composition, but from the point of view of a writing pro it's probably hopelessly bad. "A review of our records indicates . . . Our completed investigation

reveals . . . Thanking you in advance for your kind cooperation . . ."
I doubt very much whether any professional writer could bring himself to put such jargon on paper. In fact, in all my business correspondence with publishers' editors, I never found a single one who
used this kind of English.

So what you're going to get in this book is *not* "more of the same"—
correct grammar, good English, mistakes to avoid—but a new and
different way of approaching the whole problem. When you've finished
this book, I want you to answer the next morning's mail conscious
that you've abandoned your present bad writing habits and turned
over a new leaf. If you've made improvements in just a few things
you used to do wrong, that's not good enough. You should feel like
having made a New Year's resolution—quitting smoking or taking
off twenty-five pounds—and sticking to it, come hell or high water.
And you should get a daily kick out of this triumph over your old,
incompetent self.

Learning how to write, I'd tell my students, is like taking a course
in public speaking. I'd ask whether anyone in class had ever taken
such a course. Invariably a few hands would go up.

"What did you learn in that course?" I'd ask.

"Well, the main thing was learning how to face an audience . . .
not to be inhibited . . . not to be nervous. . . ."

Exactly. When you take a course in public speaking nowadays, you
don't hear much about grammar and vocabulary. Instead, you're
taught how not to be afraid or embarrassed, how to speak without a
prepared script, how to reach out to the live audience before you.
Public speaking is a matter of overcoming your long-standing nervous
inhibitions.

The same is true of writing. The point of the whole thing is to
overcome your nervous inhibitions, to break through the invisible
barrier that separates you from the person who'll read what you wrote.
You must learn to sit in front of your typewriter or dictating machine
and reach out to the person at the other end of the line.

Of course, in public speaking, with the audience right in front of you, the problem is easier. You can look at them and talk to them directly. In writing, you're alone. It needs an effort of your experience or imagination to take hold of that other person and talk to him or her. But that effort is necessary—or at least it's necessary until you've reached the point when you quite naturally and unconsciously "talk on paper."

The pros do this automatically whenever they get down to the job of writing. But it isn't a special talent you're born with—it's an acquired skill. You too can learn it—just as thousands and thousands of ordinary, tongue-tied people have learned to stand up before an audience and talk to them for five or ten minutes without making a complete mess of it.

I'll go into all the details—the tricks of the trade—in the later chapters of this book. You'll read about what to do about your words, sentences and paragraphs and, what's more important, how to convey your thoughts and feelings to the reader so that they'll come across. But before we plunge in, I'll illustrate what you'll learn with two brief examples.

Let's first take an answer to a letter of complaint. Suppose Mrs. Josephine O'Brien has an account with a chain drugstore where she's a steady customer. Every month she gets a statement with a bundle of last month's sales slips. One month she comes across a sales slip for $2.50 that says "Candy." Since Mrs. O'Brien isn't in the habit of buying candy at her drugstore, she looks at the sales slip more closely and finds that the scrawled name on top says "Obrinsky" rather than "O'Brien." So she deducts $2.50 from her check and sticks in a note, complaining that she was charged $2.50 she didn't owe and adding that she never bought a single box of candy at the store.

Now if that drugstore chain sends out typical twentieth-century American letters, Mrs. O'Brien will get an answer somewhat like this:

Dear Mrs. O'Brien:

    In reply to your recent communication, please be advised that an investigation was made which revealed that an item in the amount of $2.50 was inadvertently charged to your account due to a bookkeeping error in our Accounting Department. A cancellation of the above entry has been effected.

Very truly yours,

There are so many things wrong with this letter that I can't go into all of them right now. Let's just hit the high spots:

1. It calls Mrs. O'Brien's complaint letter, rather contemptuously, "your recent communication"—as if she were a supplicant addressing the high and mighty company on bended knees.

2. It uses the stale old cliché "please be advised." Every single textbook in business-letter writing says "please be advised" is utterly taboo.

3. It says, pompously, that "an investigation was made"—meaning that someone took a minute and a half to look things up.

4. It says the investigation "revealed" something, as if the $2.50 error had been a closely guarded state secret, now at long last exposed to the public gaze.

5. *It never admits that Mrs. O'Brien is right and the company has made a mistake.*

6. It says the error was made by "our Accounting Department"— implying that the company itself was wholly free of blame and the culprit was some poor wretch of a bookkeeper, who was instantly fired without pension or severance pay.

7. It says that "a cancellation of the entry has been effected," but leaves Mrs. O'Brien still in doubt whether her account has been credited with the $2.50 or whether she'll be hounded by a crescendo of dunning letters for months and months to come.

And so on. You see how nasty modern business writing really is? Let's get the bad taste out of our mouths and read what a good correspondent might have written instead:

Dear Mrs. O'Brien:

You're quite right, of course—the $2.50 for a box of candy should have been charged to Mrs. Obrinsky's account rather than yours. We can only apologize most sincerely for this error and are much obliged to you for spotting it. Not many of our customers are as careful as you are in going over our bills.

We've given you credit for the $2.50, which will appear on your next statement. And we've taken steps to make sure this kind of thing won't happen again. From now on, every sales slip *must* contain the customer's initial, name and address. We'll check on this frequently.

Again, I do hope you'll forgive us for our mistake.

Incidentally, you say you've never bought our Martha Jeffreys candies. Why don't you sample a box? I'm sure you'll like them.

Sincerely yours,

I don't mean to say this is a masterpiece of letter writing or *the* solution to the problem. Others might write such a letter in dozens of different ways, all equally good. But the thing that's absolutely necessary is that someone takes Mrs. O'Brien's complaint seriously, thinks about what to say to her, and then says it openly and pleasantly.

You may say that it's easy to criticize business letters addressed to individual customers. Naturally, answers to customers' complaints are more difficult to write than routine letters to other companies on run-of-the-mill business matters. Would I apply the same approach to those?

Yes, I certainly would. Let's take a trivial item—the kind of letter thousands of companies send each other every day of the year. Let's study a covering letter to go along with an enclosure.

Suppose Amalgamated owes money for some merchandise they've bought from United, but lost the original invoice. So Amalgamated writes United and asks for a copy. United sends the copy with, of course, a covering letter. Typically, the covering letter says:

Dear Sirs:

This will acknowledge receipt of your advice dated April 10, 1971, in which you requested us to send you a copy of our

Invoice dated February 26, 1971, No. 3756981, for 3 doz. green dotted Widgets, in the amount of $350.00 plus $21.00 tax, totaling $371.00.

We are pleased to comply with your request. Please find enclosed herewith a photostatic copy of the above-mentioned Invoice, indicating the merchandise ordered and the price charged in the amount stated hereabove.

We trust that this photostatic copy of our Invoice No. 3756981 will be self-explanatory and hope that this matter will be hereby settled to our mutual satisfaction.

Thanking you in advance for your cooperation, we are

Very truly yours,

You say I'm exaggerating? Very good. You've just passed a test of your sensitivity to business jargon. I admit I've constructed this letter to contain just about all the worst elements of business jargon I could work in. I won't analyze it point by point like the other one; I'll just let it stand here as a rather gruesome monument of so-called English prose.

And what would be a *good* way of writing such a letter? Try to guess.

Should you just stick the invoice copy into an envelope and send it off by itself? No. Obviously that wouldn't do. It might get mixed up with other pieces of mail and never reach its proper place in the file.

Should you strip the letter of all the unnecessary verbiage and just say "Enclosed please find . . ."? Yes, that would be a step in the right direction, but you'd still be stuck with the hoary old cliché "Enclosed please find." Is that really necessary? Why not write it this way?

Re: Your order for 3 doz. green dotted Widgets
Our invoice 3756981, 2–26–71

Gentlemen:

Here's a copy of the invoice you asked for.

Now I see you shrinking back. Can you really do such a thing? Is this allowed? Doesn't it look awful to send a decent, respectable business firm such a one-line note? Isn't it too terse? Too curt? Wouldn't they take offense? Can you stop after just nine words? Can you start quite as casually as "Here's"? Can you end a sentence with the preposition *for*? Can you send a letter like this openly through the mails, on your own company letterhead?

Yes, you can. In fact, you should—frequently or as a daily exercise, to keep on your toes and remind yourself of your resolution to use the modern professional style of writing.

It's not so hard, really. The first time it'll hurt a little, I know. There'll be a slight but unmistakable shock to your nervous system. But by the tenth time it'll feel much better, and by the fiftieth time your nervous reaction will have disappeared.

Once, at about the twelfth session of my training course, I happened to deal with a company letter starting with the classic "Enclosed please find."

"What's a better way of saying that?" I asked the class. Together, in a happy chorus, they answered: "Here's."

At that moment, I felt proud. I knew they were on their way.

2 *Talk on Paper*

The Internal Revenue Service is *not* known for its graceful, easy-to-read style. Rather, it uses an impenetrable official jargon, covering the jungle of our tax laws with a thick fog of murky prose.

You'd think the revenue writers are so set in their ways they can't possibly come up with a decent English sentence, addressing the poor suffering taxpayer as if he were a fellow human being. But you'd be wrong. When the Revenue Service finds itself unarmed, so to speak, and bereft of its heavy legal artillery, it can be almost as ingratiating and persuasive as a door-to-door salesman.

I'm a free-lance writer and pay my estimated income tax each year in quarterly installments. Since free-lance earnings are hard to estimate in advance, I sometimes underestimate what I'm going to make. The tax law says that if my estimate falls below 80 percent of my actual income, I have to pay a penalty—6 percent interest on what I *should* have paid.

Last year I was a pessimist and paid less than I should have. So, a few months later, the Revenue Service sent me Form 4177, softly titled "about your estimated tax payments" and asking for a "proposed addition to tax." Mind you, I wasn't in arrears and this was no cold, unfriendly deficiency notice. Rather, I was someone who may have underrated his income for perfectly good legal reasons and was therefore entitled to some courtesy. So the form letter began like this:

In reviewing your income tax return for the above year we find you apparently did not pay as much of your tax on a current basis as the law requires. It's possible, of course, that you have made payments we haven't credited to your account. If this is the case, please let us know of any error. And accept our apology for the inconvenience caused you.

Now the tone of this letter wasn't perfect by any means. They shouldn't have said "reviewing" and "above" and "apparently" and they should have changed a few other things. But they *did* use the contractions "it's" and "haven't" and they started the last sentence rather nicely with "And." On the whole, the letter showed the Internal Revenue Service willing to unbend and trying, shyly and awkwardly, to greet the customer with a smile.

As far as I know, Form 4177 is unique among the form letters of the Revenue Service. Perhaps they hired professional help from the outside to do this uncongenial job. At any rate, the way it's written betrays the hand of a pro. Whoever wrote it knew that you have to use "spoken" English to get results.

Well, when even the Internal Revenue Service stoops to writing like this when they think they have to, it surely shows that the ability to "talk on paper" is indispensable for good, effective writing. If you don't know how to do this—if you're inhibited, or hampered by what you learned in school or college—then you have to learn how to do it step by step, until eventually it becomes second nature. Nothing can possibly make you a good writer if you haven't mastered the art of written talk.

Your first and most important step is simply to use your imagination. Try as hard as you can to think of the addressee of your letter or report as if you talked to him or her on the phone or across your desk. Be informal. Relax. If Mr. O'Connor or Mrs. Lopez were on the phone or sitting right in front of you, you'd talk to them in your ordinary voice and with your ordinary manner, vocabulary, accent and expression. You wouldn't say "please be advised" or "we wish to inform you." You couldn't possibly get out the words—not with Mrs. Lopez or Mr. O'Connor looking at you or listening to your voice, expecting language that resembles normal human speech. Instead, you'd say something like "you see, it's like this" or "let me explain this to you, Mrs. Lopez" or "yes, Mr. O'Connor, I understand how you feel."

Many of my students have found it helpful to use other little mental aids. The trick is to remind yourself of talk in a conversational tone, in informal surroundings. Try to imagine yourself talking about *this* subject to *this* person at lunch, across a cafeteria or restaurant table. Punctuate your sentences, in your mind, with a gulp of coffee or a bite from a sandwich. Intersperse your thoughts mentally with an occasional "you know" or just simply "Joe." Can you say "If there are additional infractions, Joe, we shall have no alternative but to request that you make other banking arrangements"? Of course you can't.

So write as you talk. Talk, talk, talk on paper. Go over what you've written and try to listen to it. Does it sound like talk? If not, change it until it does. Letters, in this day and age, are only poor substitutes for talk over the phone. In a few years we'll probably have video phones available to everyone. Can you imagine people speaking "business English" over such a phone while the other fellow is watching?

Have I convinced you? Are you ready to try? Are you willing to learn how to put talk on paper? All right, here we go. There are seven ground rules—seven specific style devices that'll make your written language look and sound like spoken English, taken down in shorthand or with a tape recorder and transcribed for people to read. Here they are:

THE SEVEN GROUND RULES

1. Use contractions like *it's* or *doesn't*.
2. Leave out *that* whenever possible.

    3. Use direct questions.

    4. Use the pronouns *I, we, you* and *they* as much as possible. Avoid using *it* and the passive voice.

    5. If possible, put prepositions at the end.

    6. When you refer back to a noun, repeat the noun or use a pronoun. Don't use "elegant variation."

    7. Don't refer to what you *wrote* or are going to *write*, but to what you *talked about* or are going to *talk about*. Don't use such words as *above, below* or *hereafter;* instead, say *earlier, later, from now on.*

Let me explain these seven rules in detail. First of all, let's have a look at contractions. There are fifty that are commonly used in writing. Here's the list:

I'm, I've, I'll, I'd
you're, you've, you'll, you'd
he's, he'll, he'd
she's, she'll, she'd
it's, it'll
we're, we've, we'll, we'd
they're, they've, they'll, they'd
aren't, isn't, wasn't, weren't
haven't, hasn't, hadn't
won't, wouldn't, shan't, shouldn't
can't, couldn't, mustn't
don't, doesn't, didn't
here's, there's, where's, how's, what's, who's
that's, that'll
let's

Occasionally I've also seen *this'll, who've, who'd* and *there'd.* But don't let yourself get carried away and write *should've* or *it'd* or some other odd-looking contraction that'll startle the reader. Stick to my list of fifty and you'll be doing fine.

Now you'll ask, Should I use these fifty contractions every single time the opportunity comes up? The answer is no. You have to go by feel. Sometimes you would say *it's* and some other time, in the normal flow of your own speech, you would say *it is*. (Note that in this very sentence I said twice "you would" rather than "you'd." Why? Because that's the way I'd have said the sentence aloud if I'd been talking to you.)

In general use contractions freely. If they don't show up in your writing the first time, revise the first draft and put them in. (Learning this new way of writing will mean a lot of revising and rewriting, I know. That can't be helped. It's like learning French or Spanish or German or *any* new language. You can't expect to switch to contraction writing from one day to another after you've carefully avoided them in writing all your life.)

So write *don't* and *it's* and *haven't* and *there's*. Practice. Do it again and again and again until you acquire the habit. In fact, you'll probably never acquire the habit completely and will never use contractions at every single occasion where they'd fit in. You'll find that for the rest of your life you'll fight a continuing struggle to stick to your informal writing style. It's much like staying off cigarettes.

Nevertheless, the battle has to be fought. There's nothing that's so important for improving your writing style as this seemingly trivial business of using contractions. It's the entering wedge. Once you've learned this basic trick of all professional writers, then at least you can start producing prose on paper that will be clear and informal and effective.

The first few times will be hard. As I said before, your writing style is the product of nervous habits and inhibitions that have been reinforced daily since your early school days. You'll have to work at it, and work hard. After the first few times, it'll come easier. Eventually, you'll rather enjoy this new way of expressing yourself on paper.

But meanwhile you have scruples and compunctions and hesitations. Can you write like this on all occasions? What will your boss or supervisor say when he sees you breaking out in this free-and-easy manner? How will the addressees of your letters feel, and the readers of your reports?

The answers to these questions are simple. (I've given them hundreds of times in the classroom.) Don't be afraid. Most likely, nobody will notice this astounding change in your writing style. If they do, people probably will like it and approve of it; after all, most of them are normal people just like you and me, who speak with contractions and read them every day in their newspaper. If you do run into criticism—particularly from your supervisor or boss—well, you'll just have to fight it out. Maybe you can convince him and, if not, you've at least shown that you take your work seriously and are trying to improve it.

So don't be afraid. Nothing will happen to you if you go with the times. Chances are, in fact, that your improved written work will make a good impression where it counts. Hundreds of people in my classes have since climbed the ladder of promotion; some of them, years later, have sent me their departmental employees so *they* would learn how to write the new way.

Another question that always comes up with contractions is this: How about the kind of writing that is *meant* to be stiff and formal? Can you—and should you—use contractions in a dunning letter, for instance, or in a legal document?

Well, let's look at a dunning letter. Here's a paragraph from an actual letter:

> It is imperative that you submit the above amount within five days. Failure on your part to comply may result in legal action at your expense.

Now let's put in the contraction *it's:*

> It's imperative that you submit the above amount within five days. Failure on your part to comply may result in legal action at your expense.

Is this an improvement? Obviously not. In fact, the word *it's* in the second version sticks out like a sore thumb and gives the whole paragraph a sort of wolf-in-sheep's-clothing effect.

But does that mean you should abstain from contractions in all dunning letters and all writing you want to be taken seriously? Not at all. I won't allow you that excuse. If contractions don't fit in with the rest, it simply means that the rest of your writing should be rewritten in such a way that contractions *will* fit in. In other words, you should use contractions because they'll force you to use all the other style devices you'll learn in the rest of this book. It's true that you can't write "It's imperative that you submit . . ." because it doesn't sound right. But you can, and should, write something like this:

> If you don't pay this amount within five days, we'll start legal action at your expense.

Now which, do you think, is more effective—the original version or this one? I'm firmly convinced it's this one. Contractions in a nice and friendly letter sound nice and friendly, but contractions in an unfriendly letter sound blunt and menacing. The slow-paying customer who gets the "It is imperative" letter may shrug his shoulders and go about his business. But the customer who reads "If you don't pay we'll start legal action" will perhaps be scared enough to pay up.

Or take an official legal document like a will or a sales contract. Of course it would be highly unusual to say "It's my intention to bequeath . . ." or "The buyer agrees he'll pay in monthly installments . . ." But would the world come to an end? It would not. All that would happen is that a lawyer would have learned to express himself in a little more lively English. Legally, the change wouldn't make any difference whatever.

So use contractions. They're the Number One style device of modern professional writing; they're also the Number One training device for you, the person who wants to learn. You're lucky the English language has this clear distinction between informal and formal language. French doesn't have it—in French contractions must *always* be used. German doesn't have it either—if you use contractions in German writing, it means you're imitating some dialect or regional speech.

As far as I know, *no* other language has exactly what English has—contractions that show clearly that you're using informal, "spoken" English. It's an invaluable resource for anyone who writes. Don't deprive yourself of it.

Have I said enough? I hope so. And I hope I haven't sounded too preachy either. Just remember that contractions are absolutely essential. Even the shortest letter, of one or two paragraphs, should have a few of them.

Now let's move on to Rule No. 2: *Leave out* that *whenever possible.*

Let's say, for example, you've written the following sentence: "We suggest that you send us your passbook at least once a year." Now take a pencil and strike out *that*. This changes the sentence to: "We suggest you send us your passbook at least once a year." Isn't this better and smoother? The English language, it so happens, has the immensely practical device of leaving out the word *that* whenever you can express the sense of your sentence without it. And since *that* is one of the most frequently used words in the language, there's an opportunity to do it in almost every paragraph you write.

Again, this is something we do all the time in speaking but, except for seasoned professionals, almost never in writing. It's something you have to learn by continuous daily practice, crossing out *that*s again and again and again. "We find that your account has been overdrawn . . ." Make it "We find your account has been overdrawn." "You say that the shipment has not arrived . . ." Make it "You say the shipment has not arrived." "We agree that the statement was in error . . ." Make it "We agree the statement was wrong." And so on. Ten times. A hundred times. Until it comes automatically.

Grammatically, *that* can be a relative pronoun, an adjective or a conjunction. But you don't have to bother with that distinction. Whenever it sounds right to leave it out, leave it out. You'll always get a better, more fluent, more "spoken" sentence. Like this example I picked from yesterday's paper—a sentence with *two that*s in it: "John Loring said that he was confident that the big mutual fund would continue to rank high." Without the two *that*s this becomes: "John Loring said he was confident the big mutual fund would continue to rank high." Feel the difference? I hope you do—and I hope from now on you'll look sharply at each *that* in each of your sentences, ready to cut it out if it can't justify its existence.

While you're hunting for *that*s you should also go on a *which* hunt. (I apologize for the bad pun, but over the years I've found that students remember this business best when they're told about the *which* hunt.) Why should you go on this *which* hunt? Because more often than not, you can replace *which* by *that* or you can leave it out altogether. For example: "The agreement *which* we signed runs for five years." Change *which* to *that* and you get: "The agreement *that* we signed runs for five years." Next step, leave out *that:* "The agreement we signed runs for five years."

This may seem to you simple and obvious, but I can assure you I've found students surprisingly stubborn about it. Why this is so, I don't know, but some people love to pepper their pages with *which*es. So, although I hate to bother you with this, I'll explain the basic grammatical principle. It has to do with the difference between restrictive (defining) and non-restrictive (commenting) relative clauses. A restrictive clause is one that restricts the meaning of a noun to just one specific case, like "the tie that I saw in the window." A non-restrictive clause is one that adds some casual comment, like "the tie in the window, which is gross and disgusting."

Now, as you'll have noticed, the pronoun for a restrictive clause is *that* and the pronoun for a non-restrictive clause is *which*. Non-professional writers, of course, don't care about these distinctions—you probably have never heard of it in all your life—and use *which* all over the place. For some reason or other, they think *which* is the more elegant and dignified pronoun.

That idea is wrong. *Which* is a poor word to use where it doesn't belong. So, I repeat, go on a *which* hunt. Root it out wherever *that* would do a better job. You'll be surprised how much this will improve your style.

Next, Rule No. 3: *Use direct questions.*

Again, let's get back to that lunch-table conversation. A one-sided speech in itself is an unnatural situation. The normal, everyday kind of spoken language takes place between at least two people, with one holding forth for a sentence or two and the other interrupting with a question or some other natural response. If you listen to people talking, you'll hear innumerable questions, beginning with "How are you?" and "What you been doing?" to "What's that?" and "Really?" and "Is that so?" and "What do you mean by that?" and "How many were there?" and "What did *she* say?" and so on, endlessly. Direct questions are an essential part of the spoken language. A true conversation without questions is almost inconceivable.

In writing, of course, you have an unnatural situation to begin with. You're alone, you're putting words on a piece of paper, and somebody, some time later, is going to read what you wrote. Which makes it even more important that you should break into a direct question whenever there's an opportunity, just to *make* it sound more like talk.

I've gone over thousands of student papers, and I've formed the habit of glancing through them quickly to see whether I can spot a wiggly question mark, or two, or three. If I find them, then I know this student is catching on to what I've been teaching. The normal American adult, untouched by training in writing, simply doesn't think of using direct questions. He writes in straight declarative sentences, with a neat period after each, following each other in a steady, unbroken series.

I don't mean to say you should drag in questions by hook or crook or use rhetorical questions that don't call for an answer. Not at all. There's plenty of opportunity, in almost every piece of writing, to express what is *actually* a question in the form of a *grammatical* question, with a question mark at the end.

Look, for instance, at this sentence, which appeared at the end of a letter: "I trust you will find it possible to pay me a visit in Miami the first of next week and see more of my work." If the writer had talked to the addressee of the letter by phone, he'd doubtless have said: "How about coming down to Miami the first of next week?" or something like that. So why not *write* it as a question?

Or take another concluding sentence: "Your questions and comments are invited." Again, this is really a question: "Do you have any questions or comments? If so, please let us know."

But you don't even have to go that far out of your way. Look at your writing, and you'll find there are indirect questions—beginning with *whether*—all over the place. Make each of them direct; put them in question form, with a question mark at the end.

"We would appreciate your advising us whether you intend reactivating this account or wish to close the account." No good. Change it to this: "Do you plan to keep this account alive or do you want to close it?"

"Please determine whether payment against these receipts will be in order." Wrong again. Make it: "Can we pay against these receipts? Please find out and let us know."

Lawyers, particularly, seem to have a downright horror of direct questions. Here's an example from a court decision:

Questions Presented

The issues in the case may be thus stated:

(1) Whether the Association is exempt from federal income taxes as a social club under section 501(c)(7) of the Internal Revenue Code of 1954.

(2) Whether the Association is liable for federal excise taxes on wagering pools under section 4421.

(3) Whether the Association is liable for additions to any such tax under section 6651 on account of willful neglect in filing a return.

Now why in the world didn't the judge express himself straightforwardly? Why didn't he write: "Questions Presented . . . (1) Is the Association exempt . . .? (2) Is the Association liable . . .? (3) Is the Association liable for additions . . .?"

It's a mystery to me. Anyway, if you're like most people and suffer from a question-mark phobia or declarative-sentence syndrome, get rid of it. Branch out. Decorate your pages with question marks. Reach out to your reader by raising the pitch of your voice. There's nothing like a direct question to get some feedback to what you're saying.

Next item, Rule No. 4: *Use* I, we, you *and* they *as much as possible.*

Again, this is another trick to make writing look and sound more like actual, face-to-face talk. A speaker uses personal pronouns incessantly: they're part of the give-and-take of conversation. A writer— a poor writer, that is—clings desperately to the passive voice. If he has to use a pronoun, ten to one it's the pale little word *it.*

Here, for the first time, we're up against the insidious habit of hedging. The subject will come up again and again in this book. *Everybody,* it seems, who writes for a company or organization, is afraid of taking the slightest responsibility if he can help it. He doesn't say *we,* he certainly never says *I,* and he even carefully avoids using the straightforward pronoun *you.* No, no. Everything has to sound as if nobody had said anything at all or, heaven forbid, committed himself to anything in writing. The passive voice is used throughout; everything is mysteriously done and arranged by *it.* Nobody can sue the company—it has never said anything in so many words. Oh, yes— "it was suggested," "it appeared," "it seemed," "it was necessary," "a review of the records indicated." But all of this may have been an error, a misunderstanding, a mirage, an insubstantial quirk of language that didn't commit anybody.

President Truman had a sign on his desk that said "The buck stops here." And so it is. Everyone below the level of President of the United States is forever engaged in buck-passing. There's always someone higher up who may disagree with what the writer said; so let's be careful, let's never say anything directly; let's play it safe. No *I,* no *we;* let's cling to the blessed little word *it* and the passive voice. "It is assumed . . . it will be seen . . . it is recommended . . ." On second thoughts, "it is recommended" may be too dangerous. Let's change it to "Under the circumstances it may perhaps be wise . . ."

This thing is by now so ingrained in the mind of everyone who writes for an organization that I've had trouble in my classes explaining what a passive voice is. People have lost the feeling for it; they can no longer tell a hedging sentence from a straightforward one. So, since I know from experience that a grammatical definition of the passive voice won't do much good, I'll illustrate. The following sentences are cast in the passive voice:

"At lunchtime an elevator was used by this member of the staff to reach the company cafeteria. After the customary food selection was completed, a ham sandwich was consumed, followed by a cup of coffee and a piece of apple pie. Subsequently a cigarette was smoked. After an hour had elapsed, the elevator was re-entered and taken back to the 27th floor. The subject's desk was reoccupied. In due course, work was resumed."

If this illustration is too fanciful for you, here are some more ordinary examples from my collection:

"An investigation is being made and upon its completion a report will be furnished you."

"The above-mentioned draft has been endorsed by us and is enclosed herewith."

"All mail deposits are acknowledged. The passbook must accompany all requests for withdrawals."

"Your original check was misplaced and has now come to hand as a result of our investigation."

"A system designed to improve the speed and accuracy in the processing of your cash letter remittances has been implemented. Effective immediately it will no longer be necessary to use the subject form when remitting cash letters. Accordingly, forms will no longer be supplied. Any inquiries regarding this matter should be directed to the undersigned."

I don't have to translate these sentences for you. Nothing is easier than to write "We've made an investigation," "We'll furnish you a report," and so forth. The point is that you should acquire a violent distaste for these passive-voice sentences so you'll be physically unable to put one on paper. (I wish I could invent an "aversive" technique for this, like those drugs they give alcoholics to make them gag whenever they take a drink.)

Now let me add a few words about the proper use of the words *I, we, you* and *they*. First, let's talk about the word *I*. Normally, when you're writing for an organization, there isn't too much opportunity to say *I*. You're not writing on your own behalf; your own person is not involved. However, there are exceptions to this. You certainly should use *I* whenever you express feelings and thoughts that are your own. Often it's better to say "I'm sorry" or "I'm pleased" than "we're sorry" or "we're pleased." Sometimes the personal, individual touch will make all the difference in the effectiveness of a letter.

Certainly you can't address a man as "Dear Bob" and invite him to lunch without using the word *I*.

And my life insurance company, which has the ridiculous habit of sending me birthday cards, should surely let the agent send the good wishes in his own name.

Otherwise, when you're writing on behalf of your organization, say *we* and *us*. *Don't* use the passive voice; *don't* imply that everything is done by the impersonal workings of mechanical forces, untouched by human hands.

As to the addressee, call him *you*. That may seem obvious, but if you look at my examples more closely, you'll find that *you* is missing in a number of places where it would come naturally. "The passbook must accompany all requests for withdrawals" means "When you want to withdraw some money, please be sure to send us your passbook." Or again, "Any inquiries regarding this matter should be directed to the undersigned" means "When you write about this matter, please address your letter to me personally."

The word *they* is in a slightly different category. It's another of those telltale words that distinguish spoken and written English. In speaking, we all say "I called the telephone company and they told me . . ."

or "I went to the supermarket, but they were out of rye bread." But in writing, a company or organization is formally referred to as *it*. "We received notice from Northwestern Products that it has commenced manufacture of the equipment . . ." "The Oklahoma State agency re-evaluated the claim. In its review . . ." Well, break the habit. Stick to your resolution to write spoken English. Say "We received notice from Northwestern that *they* have commenced . . ." and "The state agency re-evaluated the claim. In *their* review . . ."

To sum up, make your writing as personal as possible. Do this and you'll follow the current trend. In a country where supermarket check-out girls wear tags with "Cynthia" or "Mary Lou," where bank tellers work behind plates that say "Mrs. Nussbaum" or "Mr. Rogowski," where everybody in shop or office is on first-name terms so that people hardly remember Al's, Dave's or Fran's last name—in such a country it's downright ridiculous to stick to stiff, buttoned-up impersonality in writing.

Twenty years ago, when I first started giving training courses at one of our largest banks, the male employees had to wear white shirts and ties. Today, wherever I go, I see offices full of men with beards and open sport shirts and women in blue jeans with long, flowing hair. The time has come to write open-shirt-and-blue-jeans prose.

Now let's go on to Rule No. 5: *If possible, put prepositions at the end.*

I know there are still millions of people in this country to whom this is a shocker. Just the other day I worked with a young editor who was upset when I changed "the clause to which I referred" to "the clause I referred to." "What's wrong?" I asked her. "Oh, I don't know," she answered. "It makes me feel uneasy."

And that's precisely the point. People of all ages were trained in elementary school and high school to avoid putting a preposition at the end, and so for the rest of their lives they're conditioned that way. Their nervous system has been permanently afflicted with a preposition-at-the-end phobia.

Quite probably, you feel the same way. And yet, it's all a myth, a superstition, a rule that's totally without scientific foundation. For some fifty years now, English-language experts have unanimously insisted that a preposition at the end is fine and dandy, while schoolteachers have been telling their pupils they should never commit such a wicked crime.

The bible of all professional writers is *A Dictionary of Modern English Usage* by H. W. Fowler. Here's what Fowler says in his 1926 edition about the preposition at the end: "It is a cherished superstition that prepositions must, in spite of the incurable English instinct for putting them late, be kept true to their name and placed before the word they govern. 'A sentence ending in a preposition is an inelegant sentence' represents a very general belief." Then follows a long article defending the preposition at the end enthusiastically and citing examples from Shakespeare and the Bible to Thackeray and Kipling.

In 1965 a second edition of Fowler's dictionary was published, revised by Sir Ernest Gowers, an English scholar who died a few years later. Gowers slightly amended Fowler's statement: "It *was once* a cherished superstition," he wrote, "that prepositions must be kept true to their name and placed before the word they govern in spite of the incurable English instinct for putting them late. 'A sentence ending in a preposition is an inelegant sentence' represents *what used to be* a very general belief, *and is not yet dead.*"

From what I've learned in my classrooms, Gowers was too optimistic. In the United States at least, as of 1972, the old superstition is very much alive. In fact, I've found it one of the most stubborn of all bad writing habits.

If you have that habit, train yourself rigorously to put the preposition at the end whenever it feels right to do so.

Instead of "The hearing examiner decided that the claimant was not entitled to the benefits for which he applied" write "The hearing examiner decided the claimant wasn't entitled to the benefits he applied for."

Instead of "It has been determined that new employees are only introduced to those individuals with whom they are initially assigned" write "We've found that new employees are introduced only to those they're first assigned with."

In short, a preposition *is* a good word to end a sentence with. And grammatical superstitions are something to get rid of.

And now we come to Rule 6: *When you refer back to a noun, repeat the noun or use a pronoun. Don't use "elegant variation."*

The term "elegant variation" was coined by Fowler in *Modern English Usage*. His article about it is perhaps the most famous in his famous book. It's reprinted unchanged in the second edition, since "elegant variation" is still very much in fashion. People do it all the time. Almost all my students were addicted to it, and probably so are you.

To illustrate, I'll quote two recent examples from the *New York Times:*

1. "The Dow-Jones industrial average tumbled 13.14 points to finish, battered and weary, at 825.86—the lowest level of the day. This carried *the blue-chip indicator* down to its poorest close since last Dec. 23, when it finished at 823.11."

Why did the writer use the strained expression "the blue-chip indicator"? Because he was addicted to elegant variation. He felt he couldn't repeat "Dow-Jones average" (too close to his first use of the words) and he shied away from using the humble pronoun *it*. The natural way to say it would have been "The Dow-Jones industrial average tumbled 13.14 points to finish, battered and weary, at 825.86 —its lowest level of the day. This carried *it* down to its poorest close since last Dec. 23, when it finished at 823.11."

2. "No matter what Congress does about repealing the 'equal time' law that inhibits televised political debates, President Nixon reportedly has no intention of participating in such encounters in 1972. White House insiders say *the Republican incumbent* is not remotely considering offering this forum to his Democratic challenger, whoever he may be."

"The Republican incumbent"! Have you ever heard anyone refer to the President like that? Of course not. Pure elegant variation. This paragraph should have read ". . . . President Nixon reportedly has no intention of participating in such encounters in 1972. White House insiders say *he* is not remotely considering . . ." Or, instead of the simple pronoun *he,* the writer might have said "the President" or "Mr. Nixon" or "Nixon."

Let these examples be a lesson to you. Go and sin no more.

Finally, Rule No. 7: *Don't refer to what you* wrote *or are going to* write, *but what you* talked about *or are going to* talk about. *Don't use such words as* above, below, hereafter; *say* earlier, later, from now on.

The reason for this rule is simple. The basic principle is that your writing should look and sound as much as possible like a transcript of your spoken words. So, naturally, there shouldn't be any words that refer to the piece of paper you're writing on, or to some specific words or expressions *on* that piece of paper. When you write the word *above,* you direct the reader's eye or mind to something a little further up on the page or to something on a previous page. But when you write the word *before,* you cast his mind back *in time* to something you said earlier.

For as long as there's been writing and printing, people who drafted written documents have used words referring to other words appearing *above* or *below,* or to the document as a whole—*herein, herewith, hereby*—or to other documents—*wherein, whereby.* So these words, and all others like them, have taken on an old-fashioned, Victorian or even eighteenth-century flavor. They'll turn every piece of writing instantly into a fake antique.

Let me digress here for a minute. In my own mind, these words—like *aforementioned, hereafter, said, such, the undersigned*—conjure up the picture of my father's old law office in my native Vienna.

My father bought his law practice from an older lawyer's widow in 1905. With the practice came the office and living quarters, combined in the same apartment, plus two or three of the old employees. I remember the outer office as it looked when I was a small boy. There were tall wooden file cases along the walls, with heavy wooden sliding doors, behind which the clients' files lay on shelves. There was a stand-up desk, on whose slanted top lay the gigantic open daily journal, in which all trial dates and appointments were entered by hand. There was Herr Steinschneider, the old white-haired law clerk, who was a hunchback with a perpetually dour expression. And in the corner there was that perennial attraction to a small boy, an old copying press.

I'm sure you've never seen a copying press, except perhaps in a museum, so I'll describe what it looked like. There was a tremendously heavy cast-iron base, about three feet square, upon which rested an equally heavy square top. In the center there was a vertical bolt with a three-foot-long horizontal bar sticking through it. You operated the press by turning the bar clockwise with both hands until you'd screwed the top and bottom tightly together. Inside, of course, you had your documents, prepared in fancy longhand script and inked specially for copying. The whole monstrous machine was painted in fire engine red.

I'm describing this old copying press deliberately because I want you to remember it whenever you're tempted to use those old nineteenth-century reference words in your writing. They belong to the same era. Think of old Herr Steinschneider using his copying press before you put any of them on paper.

Here's a list of the words you should *not* use for reference:

> *above, above-mentioned, above-captioned*
> *aforementioned, aforesaid, aforegoing*
> *captioned, subject*
> *below*
> *such, said, same*
> *hereafter, hereby, herein, hereinafter, hereinbefore, hereof, here-*
> *to, hereunto, herewith*
> *thereafter, thereby, therein, thereof, thereto, thereunto, therewith*
> *whereby, wherein, whereof*
> *the latter, the former*
> *the writer, the undersigned*

What should you say instead? Simple: If you're referring to something you just mentioned or are about to mention, say *this* or *these*. For instance, instead of "the above-captioned matter" say *"this* matter." Instead of "The facts are as described below" say "The facts are *these."*

Instead of *such, said, same,* say *the* or *it.* For instance, instead of "such agreement having been signed" say *"the* agreement was signed." Instead of "said building owned by" say *"the* building owned by." Instead of "Please return same" say "Please return *it."*

Instead of *hereinafter* say *from now on.* Instead of *thereof* say *of it.* Instead of *wherein* say *in which.* And instead of *herewith* say nothing —change "enclosed herewith" to "enclosed." (Or, as I said before, say "Here's.")

Finally, instead of "the writer" or "the undersigned," say "I."

I've seen thousands of business and government papers disfigured by those dusty, musty words. But I was really shocked the other day when I saw a plan for programming computer-written legal correspondence, filled to the brim with *herein*s, *whereas*es and *inasmuch*es. Here's a sample:

> Dear Sirs:
>
> Reporting on the above-captioned account that was previously referred to this office for collection, we regret to advise that this debtor has ignored all our demands for payment of this account.
>
> Whereas it does not appear that collection will be effected without the institution of suit, and if it is desired that we proceed with legal action, please forward itemized bills in triplicate.
>
> We now await your reply and authorization as outlined herein.

This moth-eaten language, as I said, is proposed to be fed into computers and distributed in vast numbers. God help us! If Victorian business jargon is now to be frozen into our sophisticated hardware, then there's really no longer any hope for the English language.

Perhaps you who're reading this have the responsibility of drafting form letters or programming computers. If so, please give some thought to the consequences of your work. Instead of the letter I just quoted, write something like this:

Gentlemen:

We've written three collection letters to this customer, but got no answer. We think it's time to sue. If you agree, please send us three copies of your itemized bills so we can go ahead.

We'll keep you posted.

3 Get the Facts

Last August I got the following letter, slightly changed, from a publisher:

Dear Mr. Flesch:

We plan to publish a college textbook entitled *College English Skills,* Revised Edition, by Leslie Thompson, Lowell Jacobsen and Edward L. Saintsbury in March 1972. This is a 40 percent revision. A softbound, it will retail for $4.95 and contain 480 pages.

May we have your permission covering markets in the United States and Canada to include the following selection:

"How to Be a Perfect Speller" from *Saturday Review,* Jan. 14, 1961, from "Spelling is the stepchild of our scientific age . . ." to ". . . *deign* and *disdain* within a few pages of his dictionary."

There is a possibility that the market for this textbook will be enlarged to world in the English language. Could you please quote the additional fee, if any, required to cover the British markets.

We have received permission from *Saturday Review.* A copy of the book will be sent to you at the time of publication. Thank you for your time and cooperation.

This covers everything, doesn't it? The letter is stuffed like a sausage with all the pertinent facts—the book, the authors' names, the price, the excerpt wanted, the proposed markets, the offer to send a copy of the book—what else is there?

When I got around to answering the letter, I found out. The writer had left out the most important fact of them all—how many words he wanted to buy. Fees for reprint permissions are based on the number of words to be reprinted, and that key item was missing.

Perhaps you'll say that, after all, the writer of the letter did give the opening and closing words of the wanted excerpt and so I could easily find out for myself how many words there were in between. But in fact I could not. When I got the letter, I was at our summer cabin in Nova Scotia, a thousand miles away from my desk and my files. I remembered that ten-year-old article only vaguely and hadn't the slightest idea how long that passage was. Two hundred words? Five hundred? One thousand? Two thousand? It could be anything at all and the proper fee, of course, would vary accordingly.

In the end I sat down and asked for an amount that popped into my mind. Too much? Too little? I simply didn't know.

The moral of this tale is clear: Whatever you write, put in all the facts the reader needs to know. Do your homework. It would have taken that permissions editor maybe two minutes to count the words to be reprinted, but he was too lazy or busy to do it. Most probably, he didn't think of it. The letter to me was one of perhaps fifty letters he sent out, all written by the same formula and containing exactly the same information, except of course for the specifications of the material wanted.

But, you'll say, what has that got to do with writing? Sure, people leave out facts or make other mistakes about the contents of their letters, but that doesn't affect the words and sentences they use to convey their thoughts, does it?

Of course it does. My students are always surprised when I go into the subject matter of their work, but after some time they realize that it's necessary. Again and again I'll come upon a weak phrase or unclear sentence and ask the student, "What does this mean?"

"Oh," he'll explain, "actually I wasn't quite sure of the answer . . . I didn't have time to study this . . . I was deliberately ambiguous . . . You're right, it doesn't really mean anything."

Here again is something the untrained writer must learn from the pro. The pro—the newspaper reporter or magazine article writer—does his work on the iceberg principle. He collects masses of data and after he's done his legwork he produces his article, letting you see one-ninth of the stuff he's got. Result: A piece of writing that's solid because the writer knows eight times more than he's telling us.

The typical business or government writer doesn't work that way. Instead, more often than not, he looks at the incoming letter, glances through the file and begins dictating. "Thank you for your letter of June 26 in which you . . . er . . . [one hundred or two hundred words repeating gist of incoming letter] . . . er . . . uh . . . In reply we wish to advise . . . [shuffles through file until he finds clue to his answer] . . . er . . . [swings into standard formula answer paragraph, using exactly the same words he's used a thousand times before] . . . If you have any other questions, please don't hesitate to write to us . . . uh . . . Very truly yours."

Maybe I'm exaggerating, but most of the letters I see look as if they'd been written that way. The particular case may have all sorts of special features, but the bureaucratic answer that comes back looks like a million others and doesn't deal with specifics.

The remedy is, almost always, more facts. From time to time, I ask my students to bring in the material they worked from—the incoming letter, the court decision they had to digest, or whatnot. I'll look at these papers and I'll say, "Why isn't this marked up?"

A good writer is someone with an itchy pencil. He reads whatever he uses for his writing actively, with pencil poised, and emerges with passages marked in the margin, possible verbatim quotes underlined, question marks, exclamation points, notations—whatever will be useful to him when he gets around to his work. Source material that isn't marked deserves an F. How can anyone come up with a decent write-up if he doesn't pay attention while he's reading up on his subject? It would be like a reporter sitting through a press conference without taking notes.

Yes, you have to get the facts—and you have to get them *right.* "Spell the names right" says the old newspaper adage. You'd be surprised how important that principle is in business. Every year I get a sales letter from the automobile dealer I bought a car from in 1957. Every year my name is misspelled ("Flesh" instead of "Flesch") and in recent years, since the company has adopted the insidious habit of sprinkling my name over the whole sales letter ("We are now prepared to offer you, Mr. Flesh"), this has become particularly galling. Needless to say, I haven't bought another car from them.

And so with everything. The number of sheer mistakes that fill business and government writing is staggering. Names are wrong, dates are wrong, amounts are wrong, information is wrong. Now that we have computers, all those errors are instantly plugged into miles of tape and wiring, and it takes vastly more time and effort than it used to to get things corrected. (When the computer in Albany, New York, misspelled my wife's name on her driver's license, it took several months and a brand-new application to get things straightened out.)

Samuel Butler said, "I do not mind lying, but I hate inaccuracy." Not a bad motto for anyone who wants to improve his writing.

But suppose your facts are right. You've collected them, you've checked them again and again, and you're all set to write. You've even taken my advice to heart and used the iceberg principle—you've more facts than you can possibly use. Which of them should you pick?

At this point you're up against the difficulty I mentioned before. If it was up to you, you'd use the absolute minimum, putting on paper exactly what the reader needs to know and not one word more. You're not a writer by profession or natural bent, and when you have a choice, you'd always rather *not* write than write. So you keep your letter or report as short as possible. Brevity! you say to yourself, giving yourself a nice pat on the back.

You don't deserve it. Brevity isn't always a virtue by any means.

In fact, most business writing is too short rather than too long. Letters and reports are poor because they don't tell the reader enough. Why? Because the writer was trying to finish his chore as quickly as possible and kept to himself what he should have told the world. It's the old nervous inhibition again, the thing that keeps people tongue-tied in front of an audience, the shying away from communication. A professional writer sits in front of his typewriter and produces words in an easy flow. He knows he can always cut a sentence, a paragraph, a page, two pages—what does it matter? His words are expendable and there are always lots more where the original ones came from. But the business writer doesn't have that confidence in his ability to produce. He gets a long letter of complaint and answers it with a paragraph or two, satisfied he's done his work. The hateful job of answering a letter has been done. Next letter.

Innumerable times I've sat in training sessions and the trainees would tell me reams of fascinating, pertinent, illuminating, explanatory, enlightening stuff they somehow hadn't included in their original drafts. "Why didn't you put that in?" I've asked. "Why does all this stuff have to come out in conversation? Why did you drop it under the table?"

Of course I know the answer to these questions. It's because the untrained writer would rather keep a fact to himself than give it away.

Sometimes I've asked whether anyone in the room ever bought an item by mail because they'd read about it in a sales letter. There's always someone who's done so. One young woman bought a fruit-cake, another subscribed to a magazine. (One fellow once said he'd bought a pair of pants by mail. They didn't fit.)

"What made you buy?" I've asked. "What persuaded you?"

Naturally, it was the description of the item in the sales letter. They bought the cake or the magazine—or the pants—because the letter writer had described the merchandise in such glowing terms that they couldn't resist.

And how did he do that? Mainly by using a lot of specifics. Sales letters—which are nowadays written by seasoned pros—are *always* long. In fact, the typical sales letter you get in the mail consists of a two-, three- or four-page letter, packed with alluring facts, plus an illustrated folder or brochure, plus an order blank, plus a self-addressed envelope—just as much paper and information as the post office is willing to ship at the cheaper rate.

The letter itself always brims with attractive features. If it's something to eat, they tell you about each fancy ingredient that'll make your mouth water; if it's a news magazine subscription, they'll tell you about each sensational event that'll happen next year and you'll miss if you don't subscribe to the magazine.

And if it's records, they'll send you for instance this bundle that came just the other day from Time-Life Records: a four-page, two-thousand-word-long letter, describing in minute detail the contents of the first album of the series ("You can almost see the courtly gatherings of ladies in hoopskirts, gentlemen in powdered wigs and knee breeches who first enjoyed these gay compositions"); an enormous poster, with lavishly colored pictures showing baroque orchestras, instruments, figurines and decorations, and accompanying text describing "the silver glint of Bach's trumpets, the brittle twang of Couperin's harpsichords, the sultry warbling of Telemann's oboes, the velvet throatiness of Purcell's violins"; an oversize postage-paid order card; and, to top it all, a demonstration record with five highlights from the works of Bach, Handel, Beethoven, Tchaikovsky and Leonard Bernstein.

Why is this so? Because the mail-order advertising people found out long ago—by a great deal of solid research—that each additional fact will increase the percentage of sales. You never can tell what a prospective buyer will respond to. So you add another fact, and another, and still another. Each color picture, each fact-filled piece of paper will add to the force of the presentation.

Think of a door-to-door salesman trying to sell a vacuum cleaner or an encyclopedia. He doesn't limit himself to a sentence or two, showing what he has to offer and naming the price. Instead, he lovingly, in his prepared spiel, dwells on each individual feature, demonstrates all the attachments, and overwhelms the housewife with facts, facts and more facts.

In the same way, if you write any kind of letter that has an element of persuasion in it—or is simply trying to make a good impression on your reader—don't think you've done your job if you just state the essentials. You have to go out of your way to open up—you have to produce interesting reading material—you have to *tell* them.

So I can't urge you enough to do your homework thoroughly, get hold of all the facts you can dig up, *and put them in your letter or report*. And how do you get your facts? As I said, first of all, by mining the pieces of paper you're working from—the incoming letter, the material in the file, the sources of information—and by paying attention to every detail. If the letter to be answered was written in longhand on cheap paper—note that fact. If there's a discrepancy in dates or amounts—note that fact. If there's an unusual specification or circumstance—note that fact. If there's a telling phrase to quote back in your answer—note that fact.

If you can't get all the information you need from the papers on your desk, use the phone to find out more. Go down the hall to ask someone who knows. Use the library. Do some legwork.

Of course you'll say you don't have the time to do exhaustive research for every little letter. You have to get through the day's work and can't put too much time into each piece of writing. I realize that. But I can only tell you what would be the right way to do it. The rest is up to you or your company. To produce good writing, you should do the best you can.

And now, having said all this, I want to go one step further. Even if you follow my advice and get lots and lots of facts to put your writing on a massive invisible foundation—even that isn't enough. Facts not only have length, breadth and width, they also have a sort of fourth dimension, depth. Behind and underneath the facts and data you're dealing with, there are other things you have to guess at— intentions, motives, interpretations, the hidden meaning that has to be brought out so your reader will fully understand. It's the business of a good writer to look at his material and tell the reader *what it really means*—which is often quite different from what appears on the surface.

Let me give you an example. In a recent newspaper article I found the following statistics of income between 1965 and 1970:

Year	Average Weekly Earnings	Median Family Income
1965	$ 95.06	$6,957
1966	98.82	7,500
1967	101.84	7,974
1968	107.73	8,632
1969	114.61	9,433
1970	119.46	9,867

What do these figures mean? Well, you say, they show how the income of average Americans has gone up since 1965, showing the roughly parallel rise of average weekly earnings and median family income. Those six years were a time of rising inflation and sharp rises in wages, so there's nothing very astonishing in the figures.

Or is there? If you look at the figures a little more closely, you'll find that average weekly earnings rose from $95 to about $120, or roughly 25 percent. Median family income rose from about $7,000 to about $10,000, which is roughly 42 percent. How come there was such a big difference? You look at the figures again and do a little mental calculation. The year has fifty-two weeks, so the annual income of a wage earner in 1965 was about $5,000 (roughly fifty times $100); but the whole family made about $7,000. Where did the extra $2,000 come from? Obviously from the wife. (Of course, there may have been income from teen-age children, but that wouldn't amount to very much.) So working wives in 1965 contributed about $2,000 out of $7,000—or about 30 percent—to the family income.

Now let's look at 1970. In 1970 the husband made about $6,000 (fifty times $120) and the family as a whole made about $10,000. So the wife's contribution had risen to about $4,000 out of $10,000, or about 40 percent.

Which means that in those six years the number of working wives rose tremendously, so that in 1970 the typical American family had two wage earners—with the wife earning about two-thirds of what the husband earned. In other words, since the early or middle sixties there's been a quiet revolution in American home life and the old-style family with the husband going to work and the wife staying home is rapidly becoming a thing of the past.

The newspaper writer from whose report I took the statistical table of course saw the hidden meaning of the figures; in fact, his article brought it out very forcefully. But would the typical letter or report writer have looked beneath the surface? Would *you* have? And yet this is one of the most important elements in good writing.

Let me give you another example. This one's taken from a will. Wills of course are drafted by lawyers rather than writers and are usually distinguished by *whereas*es and *hereby*s instead of outstanding prose style. And that's precisely the reason why there are so many lawsuits every year between claimants to a testator's property. What did old Aunt Bertha mean when she wrote "I give, bequeath and devise to my beloved nieces Linda and Beverly . . ."? Did she mean that Linda's children should inherit Linda's share after her death? Or did she mean that share should go to Beverly? The will doesn't say. If the attorney who drew it up had been a better writer, he'd have included a sentence spelling out Aunt Bertha's wishes clearly and plainly. Motives and intentions are part of the facts to be covered in writing. Thousands of lawsuits might have been avoided if a good working newspaperman had collaborated with the attorney in drafting the will. The reporter would have asked, pencil poised over his notebook: "Now, Miss De Luca, do you have any further comments on this point? What exactly do you have in mind?"

For instance, there was a recent lawsuit over a clause in the will of Mrs. Anna Roth, of Springfield, Ohio, who died in 1950. The clause read: "The net income of said trust estate shall be disbursed for the purpose of providing surgical operations and hospital care in order to prevent threatened blindness, in cases of glaucoma, or in an endeavor to restore sight in cases of cataract, for the benefit of residents of

Springfield or Clark County, Ohio, who have no apparent means of their own for such a purpose."

In 1971, twenty-one years after Mrs. Roth died, the trustees went to court because the meaning of that clause wasn't fully clear. Thanks to progress in medicine, surgery was no longer the main method of treating glaucoma, which nowadays is treated with drugs. Blindness has been found to be due not only to glaucoma and cataracts but also to other diseases. And wholly destitute people in the two counties had become much rarer than in 1950. So, said the trustees, what exactly were they supposed to do with the money? Should they go beyond what the will said and spend the money for other eye disease treatments than surgery of glaucoma and cataract cases? And should they give money to people who could pay *part* of their hospital bills?

The court said yes, they could do all that. But wouldn't it have been easier if there'd been one little added sentence in Mrs. Roth's will, saying "What I've in mind is to help people who suffer from eye disease and can't pay their hospital bills"?

Sentences like this are rare in wills. They're even rarer in contracts, where ambiguous, unclear language is normally used to paper over differences between the parties. Union contracts, for instance, are likely to contain vague clauses that lead to expensive arbitration. Why? Because the parties couldn't agree and finally someone proposed some innocuous phrase that satisfied everyone because it really didn't say anything. Again, if there'd been an experienced editor sitting in the corner of the room during the collective bargaining, he might have come up with a meaningful sentence that clarified the controversial point then and there.

So, in collecting your facts to write about, don't stick to the surface. Dig deeper. If you use statistics, ask yourself what is their true significance. If you have statements by interested parties, try to discount their bias. And if you're answering a letter, always try to find the answer to the all-important question: What exactly did the writer have in mind?

Over the years I've found that this is one of the main problems in business-letter writing. There's a perennial, stubborn tendency to stick to the surface. A letter has to be answered; you read it and react to what it says. Right? Wrong. *Don't* stick to the surface; *don't* mechanically respond to the words. Rather, try to figure out what was meant. The writer of the letter had a purpose in mind. His actual words may reveal that purpose; or, on the other hand, they may not. It's your job, in your answer, to get that hidden purpose exposed to the light of day and deal with it.

For example, a customer wrote to his bank and asked that one hundred dollars from his savings account should be transferred every month to the account of his niece, who was a student at New York University. Back went the answer: We regret we can't do that since we can't withdraw money from your savings account without your specific authorization each month.

Why was this the wrong answer? Because the bank employee who wrote it didn't pay any attention to what the good uncle wanted to accomplish: He wanted to help his niece get through college. What the bank letter should have said was: We suggest you open a checking account and then we'll be glad to arrange for automatic monthly transfers.

Another example: A customer wrote from California to New York that he wanted to send the key to his safe deposit box to the bank so they could open it and send him the contents. The answer went back: Sorry, regulations forbid bank officials to open safe deposit boxes.

What would have been the right answer? That's easy: Attention should have been paid to the customer's purpose. What he wanted was clear; he wanted to get his valuables shipped to California. The bank should have said: Yes indeed, we'll be glad to help you. Do you have a friend or attorney or someone else you trust in New York City? If so, send that person the safe deposit key and a power of attorney and he'll open the box and send you the contents. Sorry we can't help you more directly.

Third example: A customer settled abroad and asked the bank to empty his savings account and transfer the money to his checking account. Again, he got the cold shoulder: We regret we cannot do what you wish; withdrawals can only be made when the savings book is presented to the bank.

All that was needed here was a simple rephrasing. Instead of starting with saying no, the bank should have started with saying yes. Yes, we'd be happy to make the transfer; all you have to do is send us the book.

Why this is so, I don't know, but business writers have an inveterate tendency to say no and give the customer as much of a brush-off as they can possibly manage. Even if the purpose of his request is perfectly clear and easily accomplished, they'll stick to the surface of his letter and figure out a way of saying no.

There was one letter in particular that I used for years in my classes for bank employees. It was written to a South American—let's call him Mr. Gonzalez—who'd drawn all the money out of his New York bank account. The letter read:

> Dear Mr. Gonzalez:
>
> We are taking the liberty of writing you today as it may have escaped your notice that your current account has been overdrawn since August 20, 1961, the debit balance today being $1.09. We have thought it best to call this matter to your attention since it may be an indication that some remittances which you have expected to have credited to your account may not have been sent, or may have gone astray. It also may have escaped your notice that when balances fall below $1,000, we charge the account a service charge of $3.00 per month.
>
> In any case, we are sure that you will wish to cover this overdraft with least delay, and we trust that we may continue to maintain your account in our Overseas Division.
>
> Very truly yours,

Whenever I discussed this letter in my classes, there emerged three groups. One group of students didn't see anything particularly wrong with it. The account may have dropped to zero because remittances *did* go astray, they said. So you couldn't simply assume that Mr. Gonzalez emptied his account deliberately. And of course the bank had to try to collect the $1.09. Regulations said that if no such attempt was made, the amount couldn't be written off. So the letter, in the form it was written, was necessary to straighten out the books.

A second group was more flexible. Yes, they agreed, Mr. Gonzalez probably did want to close his account. So the main emphasis of the letter should be on asking him whether he'd like to reactivate it. Somewhere toward the end, however, he should be informed of the $1.09 overdraft, so he could send in a check for that amount. If he was a businessman of good standing he'd want to pay his debts.

Finally, there was a small group of students who'd go farther. They wouldn't mention the $1.09 overdraft at all, but simply write a pleasant little letter, inviting Mr. Gonzalez to reopen his account. Of course he may have decided, for reasons of his own, that he had no further use for a New York bank account, but on the other hand maybe he could be persuaded to change his mind. Anyway, it was worth a try.

As you may have guessed, this third group were the A students in the course. They were right. The chances were overwhelming that Mr. Gonzalez deliberately emptied his account with the intention to close it. Checks of his may have gone astray but surely you couldn't assume mistakes by the post office or the bank when there was a far more obvious natural explanation for what had happened.

And the $1.09? As the letter itself said, Mr. Gonzalez probably had no idea the bank charged $3 whenever the account fell below $1,000. So *of course* he didn't know about the overdraft. And anyway, why write a letter making a big fuss over $1.09—"we are sure that you will wish to cover this overdraft with least delay"—when the letter itself, what with the correspondent's and typist's time, paper and postage, may have easily cost $2.75 or more? Under the circumstances, the attempt to collect that ridiculous amount was irrational and inexcusable. Mr. Gonzalez, down in South America, may well have shown the letter to his friends and associates, seriously damaging the public relations of the bank.

The Gonzalez letter illustrates a basic principle of good business writing. First make sure of your facts, then go behind the facts to look for purposes and motives—and then deal with the realities of the situation.

In other words, forget about the $1.09.

4 *Spill the Beans*

I'll start a chapter again with a letter that came in the mail.

This one was from an educational institution with whose work I'd long been familiar. They were interested in simple writing and in teaching reading—areas in which I had done a great deal of work myself.

The letter was signed by the president of the institution and ran to three pages. The whole first page was given over to extremely flattering comments about my work. The president said he'd read all my books and used them extensively with his students. Naturally, I was impressed and pleased by what he said. I wondered what all this was leading up to and turned eagerly to page 2.

Page 2 contained a long and detailed description of a new program the institution was embarking on. Obviously it was something I was greatly interested in and could well fit into. It became clear that they wanted me to work with them in some capacity—"I hope that you will play a significant role in working with us," the letter said. However, I couldn't make out exactly what I was supposed to do. Was I supposed to give lectures? Be a consultant? Serve on the board? There was something fuzzy about it all and by the end of page 2 I began to feel uneasy and vaguely disturbed.

I turned to page 3, which had only a concluding paragraph on top.

My questions were answered with a thud. I was asked to make a financial contribution.

In a way, this was the most shocking letter I'd ever received. Having spent my whole life as a free-lance writer, teacher and consultant, trying to make ends meet and keep my family in groceries, I'm simply not a person who's normally asked to make significant financial contributions to *anything*. I was wholly unprepared and that little paragraph on page 3 simply staggered me.

Maybe you've had a similar experience at one time or other. Anyway, this letter was the classic example of how *not* to organize a business letter. The basic rule is to spill the beans in the opening paragraph. The worst thing you can do is wait until the very end to tell the addressee what it's all about.

And yet I've seen thousands of business letters that were written more or less the same way. Why? What makes people hold back what they have to say, trying all kinds of tricks to hide their real purpose?

I've looked into the history of this matter and I think I know the answer. There's a natural tendency in all of us to begin at the beginning and go on to the end. When you write a letter, it's the obvious and easiest way to organize your material. The trouble is that what's easy for you is hard on the reader. He has a problem or question and wants to know whether the answer is yes or no. If he has to wait until you're willing to tell him, his impatience and subconscious resentment will increase with every word. It's unfair and discourteous to let him wait—just as it's unfair and discourteous to let someone who comes into your office wait until you look up from your desk and say hello.

The simple, natural method of telling a story from beginning to end has a long and distinguished history. It's used to this day by novelists and short-story writers and by feature-article writers for newspapers and magazines. But for the bulk of what everybody reads every day—newspaper reports on what happened yesterday and today—that method has long been superseded. In fact, it's just about one hundred years out of date. Histories of journalism will tell you that during the

Civil War news writers made a major invention: they discovered the inverted pyramid style of writing.

What is meant by that? Well, up to the 1860s papers had no big headlines and on top of each column on page 1 you'd find a simple little title like "Dispatches from Europe" or "In Congress." Then there'd be a leisurely story about the information the reporter had gathered and somewhere—on page 2 or 3 maybe—there might be a little morsel about a major vote in Congress or an important battle in Russia.

During the Civil War, when competition among papers was hot and when the newly invented telegraph would often break down in the middle of a dispatch from the battlefield, someone came up with the great innovation of spilling the beans right away. "Our army won a great victory . . ." the story began and even if the wires broke down after that first sentence, the paper could be printed and sold to eager buyers in the streets.

And so the inverted pyramid story started and it has been the standard way of writing news stories ever since. It's called "inverted pyramid" because that's the way the headlines are usually arranged, with a wide headline in the biggest type on top, followed by a narrower headline in smaller type, followed by a still narrower headline in still smaller type. The story itself is built on the same principle. There's the opening sentence or paragraph—the lead (pronounced *leed*)—summarizing briefly what happened. This is followed by two or three paragraphs giving more details, and this again is followed by more paragraphs giving more details and background. If there's room, there may be more tapering-off pieces of the dwindling inverted pyramid, each filling in more and more details of less and less interest and importance.

And that's the universal newspaper style of writing—with the exception of a handful of feature or sequence stories, building up to a surprise ending. But those are usually just little tidbits for entertainment. For all the big stories reporters use the standard upside-down technique; if they didn't they'd soon be out of a job.

Some months ago I passed the windows of Brentano's bookstore on New York's Fifth Avenue. They had some sort of anniversary exhibit of blown-up front pages of the *New York Times* with headlines of the big events of the century. The one I remember was the paper that appeared the day after the death of Queen Victoria. Its lead paragraph was simply this:

Queen Victoria is dead.

Maybe this four-word sentence will stick in your mind, as it has stuck in mine. But just in case it doesn't, I'll also reprint the opening paragraphs of a story that appeared in the *New York Post* in October 1971. It's just a random example, but it shows the inverted pyramid method very clearly and will serve as a good model:

A New Jersey woman who was distributing clothes and medicine in East Pakistan has been sentenced to two years in prison there.

Mrs. Ellen Connett, 28, of Dumont, was arrested about 10 days ago and charged with illegal entry to East Pakistan, according to the U.S. State Dept.

She pleaded guilty and asked for leniency on grounds of ignorance of the law, the State Dept. said.

Mrs. Connett and a British companion, both volunteers for Operation Omega, a relief mission, were arrested by Pakistani troops 10 miles inside the border, according to Mrs. William Langle, her mother.

Mrs. Langle said she learned of her daughter's arrest in a phone call last week from London, where Operation Omega has its headquarters. She was told her daughter was the first American to receive a prison sentence under such circumstances.

The State Dept. official said the American consul in Dacca will assist Mrs. Connett if she appeals the sentence.

[Mrs. Connett was freed a few weeks after this story appeared.]

Can you see the inverted pyramid? The first tier on top consists simply of the first sentence, spilling the beans of the story. The second tier is made up of paragraphs 2 and 3, filling in the details of the lead. Next follows the third tier, consisting of three paragraphs, giving still more details. And so on.

Perhaps you'll say, Why should this newspaper technique be used in writing business letters? The answer is clear: Because it's the universally used, successful way of conveying information. The addressees of your letters are not only used to this method, they've been conditioned to it ever since they started reading newspapers. They'll get nervous and uneasy when they're not told in the opening sentence of your letter what it's all about. Don't upset their long-established habits of taking in information. Start each and every letter of yours with a lead—and then build the rest of it strictly following the inverted pyramid principle. If you do this invariably, habitually and every single time, you can't go wrong—you'll never make a mistake like the educator who asked me for a financial contribution.

And now let's go into specifics—let me illustrate the principle by applying it to the major types of letters you may be called upon to write. (The principle applies to reports just as well, but I'll deal with them later in Chapter 10.)

To begin with, let's take the simplest kind of letter—a letter to another company or organization that contains a single item of information. Typically, such a letter reads like this:

> Gentlemen:
>
> In reference to your letter dated February 26, 1971, relating to Our Ref Jv-845742 United States Savings Bonds, we wish to inform you that the amount of $853.92 was credited to your account on January 15, 1971.

Now this is just one sentence and it does spill the beans immediately. However, it takes twenty-four words of reference data and "we wish to inform you that" until the reader gets to the meat of the information. Let's cross out everything up to that point—and let's change the remainder from the passive voice to the active voice while we're at it. Then we get:

Re: . . .

Gentlemen:

We credited your account with $853.92 on January 15, 1971.

Of course you'll immediately say you can't do that. The reference data are necessary, because otherwise the recipient of your letter won't know what to do with it. He has to have all these dates and reference numbers because he has to find the proper file so he can act on it.

Yes—yes indeed. By all means, be as businesslike as you possibly can. Observe all the rules of proper filing and docketing. But don't—I repeat, *don't*—do this in the opening sentence of your letter. Use a caption, a "Re" line. That's what it was invented for. Indulge yourself in all the reference paraphernalia you can think of. But after you've done this, use the opening sentence—the show window of your letter—for the lead. Tell them that "Queen Victoria is dead" so they'll know about it right away. If it's just one brief sentence—"We credited your account" or "Here's a copy of the invoice"—well, so what? What else is there to be said? Why waste your reader's time? Tell him what's what and then stop.

Actually, the standard beginning with an acknowledgment of the incoming letter *isn't* used because it's businesslike and proper. That's just an alibi. What really happens is that business writers start like this because they can't bring themselves to plunge right in. They need some sort of support—something to lean on—a crutch. Any piece of paper will do. If there's an incoming letter, they'll start with that. If there's no such letter, they'll start with the last letter *they* wrote. If there's no such letter either, they'll take an enclosure, an attachment, a form to fill out, a descriptive folder—anything at all, as long as it prevents them from getting to the point right away.

The nervous mechanism here is exactly the same that makes people look for a physical support when they have to make a public speech. I know the feeling well. I'm not the world's best speaker and public lecturer. I hate to go out on an empty stage. Fortunately, there's usually a lectern, on which the speaker is supposed to put his prepared speech. I never use a prepared speech or lecture, but I do use the lectern. Oh, how I use the lectern! I quickly walk up to it, grip its sides with both hands and, leaning on it hard, I begin my speech. I know this is cowardly and prevents me from gripping my audience from the word go, but I do it. I know myself and I do need that lectern.

But that doesn't mean you should follow my bad example and hang on to a piece of paper whenever you start a letter. It's a habit that can be overcome and *must* be overcome. *"Don't start with a piece of paper!"* I've told my students a hundred times—a thousand times. Eventually they do get rid of the habit. You can do it too. All that's necessary is to push the "piece of paper" up into the caption or down toward the end of the letter (where unimportant technicalities belong) and there you are. Do this fifty, a hundred, five hundred times and it'll become an acquired habit.

Almost, but not quite. There'll be days when you're tired, or have a slight cold, or are worried about something, so that it takes an effort to keep your mind on your work. You don't want to exert yourself. So you start a letter with "Thank you for your letter of March 13." After all, what harm does it do? you say to yourself.

I warn you. Don't do it. It's like the cured alcoholic's "just one drink" or the cured smoker's "just one cigarette." Before you know it, you'll be right back where you were. Whenever you find yourself reaching out for that tempting "piece of paper" to lean on, pull back. Start with "Queen Victoria is dead." Don't give in to your cowardly instincts.

And now let's get back to business. Here's another example of a simple letter that starts the wrong way. This is a letter I've used often because I think it's particularly instructive.

Re: . . .

Gentlemen:

In reference to the above collection item, which you instructed us to hold at the disposal of the beneficiary, we wish to advise that Mr. Ling has not called on us, nor have we received any inquiries on his behalf.

The above information is provided to you in the event you wish to give us any further instructions in the matter.

Very truly yours,

Again, let's cross out everything up to the words "Mr. Ling." Then the letter becomes (with a few other minor changes):

Re: . . .

Gentlemen:

Mr. Ling hasn't called on us, nor have we had any inquiries on his behalf.

Do you have any further instructions?

Sincerely yours,

You see what this does? Once all the unnecessary verbiage is cleared away, the letter becomes downright elegant. I know it always gives students a slight shock at first, when they look at the clean, functional opening "Mr. Ling hasn't called on us," but after a while they come to appreciate the sheer beauty of it. There's something about it that makes it practically a model of business correspondence.

If you don't see that, try a little harder. It's there, I assure you. Learn to like it. It took people quite a while to see the beauty of a Danish functional chair or a modern glass-box skyscraper.

Let's go on to a slightly more elaborate letter—a letter that deals with three items of information. Here's the original:

Dear Miss Svoboda:

In reference to your recent inquiry we are enclosing a signature card for the purpose of establishing a Savings Account with us. Please sign where indicated and furnish the information required.

For your further convenience and information we are enclosing a brochure describing our Savings Accounts.

Upon receipt of the completed card and your initial deposit we shall be pleased to establish an account and forward the passbook for your records.

We thank you for your interest and look forward to being of service.

Very truly yours,

Again the letter writer, true to form, opened with a reference to a piece of paper. Since the customer's inquiry was a phone call rather than a letter, he couldn't use an incoming letter; so he did the next best thing and started with a reference to the signature card. Of course a signature card is just a minor technicality, and the main point of the letter was the opening of the savings account, but the writer simply couldn't bring himself to start with *that*. He needed the signature card as a crutch.

Let's rewrite this letter in the classic inverted pyramid style. To do this, we have to turn it upside down. Paragraph 3, dealing with the opening of the account—the main point of the letter—becomes our new paragraph 1. Paragraph 2, dealing with the explanatory brochure, again becomes paragraph 2. Paragraph 1, dealing with the sheer mechanics of filling out the signature card, becomes paragraph 3. The windup paragraph 4 stays where it is.

Now let's change and add a few other things that are necessary and we get this:

Dear Miss Svoboda:

We'll be happy to open a savings account for you.

Currently our savings accounts pay 5 percent interest, compounded quarterly. You don't need to bring or mail your passbook every time you make a deposit, but we'll need your passbook and a signed withdrawal slip whenever you make a withdrawal. You'll find other information you may need in the enclosed brochure.

We'll open the account and send you your passbook as soon as you send us your first deposit. Please return to us also the enclosed signature card. Fill in each item and sign, with the name you want to use for your account, on the line marked with an X. Don't forget to put in your phone number, zip code *and social security number*. We're enclosing a self-addressed envelope for your convenience.

Thank you for choosing our bank. We look forward to serving you.

Sincerely yours,

Again I don't mean to say that this is the only possible solution to the problem. But it shows the sequence that should be followed—from saying welcome down to sheer mechanics—and it deals with substance rather than formalities. There's no point, for instance, in enclosing a brochure if you don't say at least a few words about what it contains. And while you're telling Miss Svoboda to fill out her signature card, you might as well try to forestall her filling it out incompletely, which will lead to more correspondence, more work, more bother. Anyway, tell her you're glad to have her as a customer—after all, she's responded to very expensive advertising designed with vast effort and ingenuity to *make* her come to your bank—and thank her for picking your bank rather than the competition across the street.

If Miss Svoboda had come into the branch and had sat down by the side of your desk, you wouldn't have started the conversation with "You have come in reference to your recent inquiry. Here is a signature card. Please sign where indicated and furnish the information required." Or would you?

So Rule No. 1 in starting a letter is to start right in with the main point—the answer to the question, the most important thing to get across. What happens if there's no such clear opening? Well, then you have to find one. If you're not responding to your reader's purpose or interest, but have to start a letter on your own, then you have to ask yourself what's the main thing *you* want. If you want to raise a question, start with your question. If you want to ask someone for a favor, start by asking him for a favor. If you want to get information, start by asking for information. It's as simple as that—*if* you stick to your resolution of getting to the point at once rather than fiddling around, stumbling your way through some awkward introduction.

For instance, suppose you're writing to another company asking for a favor. You need their help in collecting some data, or compiling some bibliographical reference notes, or some other little service they're not obliged to give you. If you called them up on the phone, you'd say, after introducing yourself, "We'd like to ask you a favor" or perhaps "Say, could you help us out on something?" or words to that effect. Why not start your letter the same way? The only way to get something you have no legal right to is to ask for it politely. Don't beat about the bush. Don't fill half of your letter with a long buildup and then ask them to do something for free.

Or let's say you have to tell your reader something he isn't prepared for—say you have to raise the price of your services. Again, don't hold back. Tell him right away. Begin your letter with "We're sorry but because of the recent rise in wholesale prices . . ." It'll be easier to go on once the unpleasant news is out of the way.

If you have a question, start with your question. For example, a bank has made a loan to a small manufacturing firm. The company has paid the monthly installments punctually, but hasn't filed the financial statement they were supposed to file each year by the end of January. The bank has asked for that statement twice—on June 30 and on September 30. Finally, on January 9 of the following year, they write a third letter. How does it start? You guessed it. With a reference to a piece of paper—the loan agreement:

In connection with your Monthly Payment Business Loan in the amount of $32,784.93 for a term of 30 months, granted in

October 1971, the corporation executed a Term Loan Agreement in which it was agreed that we would be provided with an annual financial statement thirty days after the close of each financial year.

On June 30th and again on September 30th we wrote you requesting the fiscal audit but received no reply to our letters. May we once again request that you forward the last fiscal statement dated December 31, 1971, at your earliest convenience.

Is this effective? No. It starts routinely with the "piece of paper" opening and then goes on to make the third request for the statement so inconspicuously that it sounds as if the bank didn't care. After all, the company pays its loan installments every month, so the fiscal statement is just a formality.

But of course it isn't. If a whole year has gone by and the company hasn't given the bank even a glimpse of its financial situation, then maybe there's something wrong. The bank, with over $32,000 at stake, has a right to know. That routine third request will never do. The letter *should* have started like this:

We're wondering why you haven't sent us your financial statement for 1971.

After that hint that the bank is getting nervous about its money, the company will start explaining things in a hurry.

(If you paid attention to what I said before in this book, you'll probably ask why my version doesn't start with the direct question "Why haven't you sent us your financial statement for 1971?" All I can say is, I didn't think that would have been right in this case. The company paid the installments and was a customer in good standing. Why offend them with a blunt direct question? All right, I'm inconsistent. I can't help that. Life isn't consistent either.)

Are there any exceptions to the basic rule of plunging right in? Yes, there are a few. If there has been some contact between you and your reader—say if you've told him over the phone what you're now confirming in writing—then of course you should hook onto that. Write "As I told you over the phone yesterday . . ." If something is general knowledge, pay him the compliment of assuming he's well informed. Say "As you know, the Federal Reserve Board recently raised its interest rate. This means that we also must charge higher rates to our customers. . . ."

If the incoming letter was addressed to someone else and you're answering it, then you have to introduce yourself first. For instance: "Our president, Mr. Marcovich, has asked me to answer your letter. I'm the District Manager for this area." Or: "The Lansing, Michigan, District Office has referred to us your letter of November 5, 1971."

If you're very late in answering, then you have to start by apologizing for the delay. Make sure you have a real, convincing reason to offer. If it's just a short delay—say up to ten days—then you'd better *not* apologize. It'll just draw attention to the late date.

Aside from these exceptions, there are *no* excuses for not starting with the main point.

Sometimes it's a little hard to figure out what should be the sequence of the inverted pyramid *after* the opening. This happens particularly when you're writing a form letter that's addressed to a variety of addressees. How do you know what's most important and interesting to them? What's most important to one person may be quite unimportant to another.

The answer to this dilemma is this. Try to find out as best you can what's most important to most people, what's second in importance, and so on. Here's an example:

There was a form letter used by a bank for people who had reported the loss of their savings book. This letter was sent out after three or four weeks to find out whether they'd found the book or not. If they'd found it, the bank would release its stop-payment order, so that the passbook owners could again withdraw their money. If the book *hadn't* been found, the bank would give them a substitute passbook.

The opening sentence of the form letter was obvious:

Have you found your passbook?

But what should come after that? Should you first deal with the people who'd found their book or with those who'd lost it permanently?

The only way to find out was to find out. I asked the students in my classes what was more common—that people who'd lost their passbooks found them again after a few weeks or that the books never turned up.

I was told that most savings books are mislaid rather than lost forever. People can't find their books and notify the bank. Then, after some time, they find the book stashed away in the back of a dresser drawer but forget to tell the bank. That's true of maybe 70 or 80 percent of the cases.

Well, then, what does this mean for our letter? Clearly this:

> Have you found your passbook?
> If you have, please let us know so we can release the stop on your account.
> If you haven't found the book . . .

I'll sum up this chapter in one sentence: *Never write a letter without first thinking up a good lead.* Newspaper and magazine writers write leads every day and I suppose the novelty and inner satisfaction of the procedure has long worn away for most of them. Still, an article writer who has thought up a particularly striking lead is apt to feel a glow of creative achievement even after he's done it a thousand times. I can promise you that you too will occasionally feel the nice inner glow that comes from having done a thing just right. And that's not a thing to be sneezed at when you're just attending to ordinary business correspondence.

I remember one occasion when I felt that glow. This was during a stint as consultant to the Social Security Administration. I worked with their writers and editors and suggested rewrites for booklets, application forms and letters. One form letter that presented a tough problem began like this:

This refers to the previously disallowed claim for HOSPITAL INSURANCE benefits which was submitted on your behalf for services received from:

Name and Address of Provider	Dates of Services

Your claim was reviewed by the medical advisory staff, and it has been determined that benefits are payable for the services rendered during the period shown above.

I can still remember my feeling of creative satisfaction when I'd finished rewriting that lead. My version was this:

You'll be pleased to learn that we're going to pay the hospital bill we first said we wouldn't. Our doctors went over your claim once more and decided you're entitled to the money after all.

5 Use Short Sentences

"What's the matter with your typewriter? Doesn't it have any periods?"

I was watching the Mary Tyler Moore show on TV. Mary played the assistant producer of a TV news show. In that particular episode there was a writers' strike and Mary had to pinch-hit as a writer. Being untrained, she naturally made mistakes and her boss, Edward Asner, corrected her copy. He immediately spotted a sentence that was much too long. And then came the line about the periods.

Obviously this was something the national TV audience would understand and appreciate. *Everybody* knows that newsmen are trained to write short, snappy sentences. Longwindedness, to them, is a cardinal sin. It's the one thing even outsiders know about the techniques of journalism. The heavy use of periods by reporters is practically an item of folklore.

The funny thing is that I'm partly responsible for this. Back in the late forties I served for a time as consultant to the Associated Press. I gave them advice on how to make their copy more readable, and the one thing that really seemed to catch on was the use of short sentences. Ever since that time American newspapers have been watching their average sentence length. In the twenty years that have passed it has dropped by about 20 percent.

Why is this so important? Because the ordinary reader can only take in so many words in one gulp before his eyes come to a brief rest at a period. If the sentence has 30 words, he may have to pause for a moment and think. If it has over 40, chances are he's been unable to take in the full meaning.

When I first collected my statistics about average sentence length in American publications, I found that in mass-circulation magazines like the *Reader's Digest* the average was 17 words. In newspapers in those days it was way beyond that—20 to 25 words—and my advice was to cut it down to at least 20.

Since then things have changed and I was pleasantly surprised when I did some checking the other day. Here, for instance, are two paragraphs taken at random from a story in the *Wall Street Journal* about the liquidation of the estate of Mrs. Dodge, widow of the auto millionaire Horace Dodge:

Dismantling her fortune may be remembered for its chaos. Most of her money is willed to members of the family, and they are squabbling in court. The unraveling is certainly complicated because of Mrs. Dodge's acquisitiveness. Just guarding her possessions since her death has been a major undertaking. Two hours after she died, about a dozen special guards moved into the mansion, and soon thereafter a barbed wire fence was thrown up around most of the perimeter of her nine-acre estate. Electric eyes later were installed around the property. Guards stay there around the clock. At night, for security purposes, the three story limestone residence is bathed in spotlights. Nobody gets through the wrought-iron gates without clearance.

Figuring out what to do with Mrs. Dodge's "things" has been a challenge to some of the best minds in the fortune-dismantling business. Previews Inc., the international real estate brokers who have convinced many Americans that broken-down castles are bargains, is trying to unload Rose Terrace. The asking price is $1,250,000. Taxes alone run $37,700 a year. The heating bill is a secret. Bob Reilly, the Previews vice president in charge of the sale, insists Mrs. Dodge's house is really "quite a bargain," because it would cost $6.5 million to build a similar mansion today, "if it could be duplicated at all."

This passage contains 14 sentences in 219 words, so the average sentence has 16 words. As you can see, this makes for good, fluent, readable writing that goes down smoothly and doesn't stop you in your tracks.

If you check the average sentence length of your own writing, you'll be in for a shock. Most likely, it runs to 20 to 25 words or even more. Writing in short, snappy sentences is a thing that has to be learned. It takes some struggle to acquire the habit.

Let's take a close look at some long, complex sentences and try to analyze what's wrong with them. I'll take my examples from an obvious source—the Internal Revenue Service. These sentences are not from their official regulations, which are meant to be read only by lawyers, but from *Your Federal Income Tax,* their annual booklet for taxpayers, "written in non-technical language."

Here's a sentence with 60 words:

> If you acquire all the substantial rights to patent property, before the invention is reduced to practice (tested and operated successfully under operating conditions) for a consideration paid to the inventor, upon disposing of your interest you may obtain the special tax treatment discussed below providing you are not the employer of, or related to the inventor, as described below.

Here's another sentence, with 64 words:

> If you are the beneficiary of an estate or trust and the fiduciary has discretionary powers to distribute all or a part of the current income, you must report all income that is required to be distributed to you (whether or not actually distributed) plus all

other amounts actually paid or credited to you, to the extent of your share of distributable net income.

Here's a third sentence, with 99 words:

> For purposes of this exception you are considered to be a full-time student during the tax year *only if* during each of 5 calendar months (not necessarily consecutive) of the tax year you were enrolled for the number of hours or courses that is considered to be full-time attendance either (1) at an educational institution that maintains a regular faculty and curriculum and has a body of students in attendance, or (2) at an on-farm training course under the supervision of an accredited agent of either a State (or political subdivision thereof) or an educational institution as just described.

You see where the writer of these monster sentences went wrong? He was a lawyer who couldn't free himself of the inveterate lawyer's habit of qualifying everything that needs qualification *right on the spot*. A lawyer thinks he can't wait with his qualifications and definitions. If he stops for a period, the reader will get away from him and not read the rest of it. He feels he has to tell the reader—*within the sentence*—what exactly each of the words means or the reader will instantly jump at the chance of misinterpreting the meaning in his own favor. In this case, he'll try to get away with paying less tax.

For instance, the tax writer reasons, if the business about "related to the inventor" isn't included in that first, 60-word sentence, there'll immediately be someone trying to save taxes by financing an invention made by a nephew. Or, if the parenthesis, "(whether or not actually distributed)," is left out of the second sentence, there'll be instant under-the-table deals with estate trustees. And if any of the 99 words were left out of the third sentence, there'd be hordes of people cheating on their taxes by taking phony mail-order courses.

As far as English composition goes, that's nonsense. If the qualifications and definitions are put in a second or third or fourth sentence, they still clearly modify the meaning of what was said before. Even from a legal point of view that's true, since no judge would rule that all legal restrictions must be packed together in single sentences or they're invalid. But I guess it's hopeless to try to cure lawyers of their bad writing habits.

The unfortunate thing is that ordinary business writers and government employees have a feeling they must write like lawyers. It's the old, ingrained habit of hedging and buck-passing. What a business writer wants most is to be safe. So he puts all his conditions and modifications into tightly packed sentences, and they get longer and longer.

The cure for this evil is to break long sentences apart at the seams. Usually it's quite easy to see where one idea leaves off and another one begins. The conjunctions *if* and *provided,* the relative pronouns *that* and *which* and other such words are good places to apply the surgeon's knife. You'll find that a 60-word sentence will normally make three sentences and a 40-word sentence two.

For instance (this is the final paragraph of a bank letter):

> If you do not resume your studies, it is necessary that you write or visit the bank to renegotiate your student loan before the maturity date by executing a renewal installment application in accordance with the required repayment terms.

There are 39 words in this sentence and two main ideas: (1) the student must renegotiate his loan, and (2) renegotiation means he must apply for renewal on the required terms. Let's split the sentence apart at the point between these two main ideas—between the words "maturity date" and "by executing." Then we get:

> If you do not resume your studies, it is necessary that you write or visit the bank to renegotiate your student loan before the maturity date. To do that, you must execute a renewal installment application in accordance with the required repayment terms.

The first of these two sentences has 26 words, the second 17. The average is 21.5.

Well, that gets us somewhere near the 20-word average, but it clearly isn't good enough. It just doesn't have the zip and snap of the *Wall Street Journal* paragraphs with their 16-word average. So let's try once more:

> If you don't resume your studies, you must write or visit the bank before the maturity date. Renegotiate your student loan. Sign a renewal installment application on the required installment terms.

I've purposely left the words more or less as they were and just speeded up the sentences. Now the first sentence has 17 words, the second 4, and the third 10. The average is 10 words.

What made the difference? How did I manage to break through that 20-word barrier? Answer: It was the simple 4-word sentence "Renegotiate your student loan." The secret ingredient was decisiveness: I said what I wanted to say in the simplest possible way and then stopped. It's the same technique that made the *Wall Street Journal* reporter write, "The asking price is $1,250,000. Taxes alone run $37,700 a year. The heating bill is a secret."

So the recipe for writing *really* short sentences (averaging well under 20 words) is to write every so often a very short sentence that says something crisply and decisively and then stops. To do that you have to be alert enough to hit the bull's-eye every few sentences or so. You can't go along in your usual fashion, answering your incoming letters one after another, stringing the same tired old phrases together, half asleep and utterly bored with your job. You've got to sit up straight, pull yourself together and pay attention. "Whatsoever thy hand findeth to do, do it with thy might," says Ecclesiastes. Sharpen your faculties. Pump some adrenaline into your system. Deal with the problem before you and solve it to the best of your ability. Have a cup of strong coffee before you start. And then watch the average sentence length of your writing drop to 16 words, or 13, or 10.

Maybe you'll say this brisk approach doesn't apply to everything. There are occasions when you don't *want* to be brisk. On the contrary, you want to be soft-spoken and subdued, trying to make your point gently and in a low voice. As in this letter:

Dear Mr. Stone:

We have noted with pleasure that for the past several months you have maintained large balances in your special checking account, and the thought has occurred to us that you might be interested in transferring from a special checking account to a regular checking account, which in all probability would incur no service charges if balances in excess of $2,000 are maintained.

I am sure that you realize the benefits of a regular checking account vs. a special checking account insofar as credit inquiries are concerned, and we would be most happy to discuss this matter with you further if you so desire.

Should you have any questions in connection with the foregoing, do not hesitate to contact me at Extension 397.

This letter is designed to be low-keyed and approach the customer with deference and circumspection. The three sentences are long and slow. The first has 62 words, the second 41, the third 19. Their average is 41 words. Can we apply the same method here and zip this letter up with one or two very short sentences? Or will that destroy its effectiveness?

No, it won't. Here's my faster version (again I'll leave the vocabulary more or less as it is):

Dear Mr. Stone:

May we make a suggestion?

We have noted with pleasure that for the past several months you have maintained large balances in your special checking account. Would you care to transfer to a regular checking account?

This would have two advantages for you. First, if you continued to keep your balances above $2,000, there would probably be no service charges. Second, as we are sure you realize, a regular account has greater prestige than a special account and would serve you better in case of credit inquiries.

I would be most happy to discuss this matter further and answer any questions. My extension is 397.

The average sentence of this version has 13 words—mainly because of the 5-word opening question, "May we make a suggestion?" and the 7-word opening sentence of the second paragraph, "This would have two advantages for you."

Isn't this much better? Isn't it better to approach the customer straightforwardly by telling him right away that you have a suggestion and then point out its two advantages for him? I think so. I think my version will get better results.

Shortening your sentences is the easiest way to improve your style. Many readers of my earlier books have found that out and have learned to break up their long sentences more or less mechanically. As you saw, this gets sentences down to an average of about 20 words, but it's hard to break through that barrier. To do that, you have to change your basic style. You have to be more direct, more straightforward, more downright. You have to write functional, stripped, clean prose. Top executives usually have a natural flair for this, and aspiring executives should develop such a style if they want to get ahead. There's an air of directness about it that stands out among the hedging, overqualified sentences usually produced by timid, cautious assistants. Which is why the occasional 4- or 6-word sentence in an employee's letter is the mark of future success. Fanciful? I don't think so. I've seen it happen too often.

One of the best students I ever had was a young man who took one of my first evening courses in writing at New York University. This was in 1946 or 1947. He'd just come out of the army and was uncertain about his future career. He got an A in my course and a short time later, when I needed a research assistant for a large project, I hired him. He worked with me for two years and then struck out on his own. In the twenty years since, he made a brilliant career and is now one of the country's outstanding consultants on fund raising.

A few months ago, apropos of nothing in particular, he sent me a report he'd written for one of his clients. I read it and was impressed by the sheer excellence of his style. No wonder he was so successful. The quality of his mind was clearly visible in his crisp, clear sentences.

Here's a sample—99 words consisting of 7 sentences with an average of 14 words:

> When questioned, most people would guess that foundations are the largest source of philanthropic dollars in America. Yet, of the $18.3 billion given away in 1970, foundations gave $1.7 billion or 9.3%.
>
> Corporations, another source usually considered prime targets in fund raising, gave $900 million or 4.9%. The average gift from corporations was 1.11% of their pre-tax profits from 1963–67 and it has not increased since then.
>
> The obvious question, then, is who did give the money? People, through individual gifts directly to recipients or through bequests. Individuals gave away $15.70 billion in 1970, or 85.70% of the total.

This is good, successful English. I'm proud that I've trained at least one person to write like that.

And this is where this chapter would end, except for the advertising copywriters. They've long ago learned to go way beyond clear, crisp 14-to-16-word-sentence English. To sell their wares, they've invented the machine-gun style.

A few weeks ago I got a letter from the bank where I spent so many years training employees in writing. But this letter wasn't written by one of those employees. It was a 4-page letter filled with high-powered advertising copy, obviously written by a seasoned ad-copy pro.

The bank was offering a subscription package of monthly tapes-plus-transcripts of discussions on the economy. Here's an excerpt of their letter:

> That's what we offer. Once each month, a taped session, about 40 minutes in length. A thought-provoking discussion. The sort of briefing you could never get anywhere else. Brain-picking, exclusive, in-depth analyses of today's—and tomorrow's—business maze. How things are . . . and how they look for the immediate future. With the chips falling where they may. Good news . . . bad news. Whatever. You'll hear it the way it is. Straight.

I took my pencil and started counting. The average sentence in this passage runs to 6 words. This is what I call the machine-gun style. The copywriter aims his language weapon straight at the prospective buyer so that in sheer panic he'll sign the order blank and take out a seventy-five-dollar annual subscription.

I think this is an abuse of the English language. The law gives a housewife three days to cancel her order for $320 worth of pots and pans after that super-dynamic door-to-door salesman has left her house. If mail-order salesmen don't relent in their verbal blitzkrieg tactics, it won't be long before mail-order buyers will have the same privilege.

Which probably will be a good thing for everyone concerned.

6 *Use Short Words (1)*

Miss Rose Willoughby was worried about her Christmas Club account. Back in November she'd instructed her bank to transfer ten dollars on the first of each month to her Christmas Club account, but she wasn't sure whether the bank had actually done it. So early in March she wrote a little note to the bank asking about it.

A few days later she got an answer. It said:

> Dear Miss Willoughby:
> In reply to your note received March 5, 1969, the Automatic Christmas Club deductions began in November 1968. Your account is up to date, and we trust this information will alleviate your concern.
> It is a pleasure to be of service to you.
>
> Very truly yours,
> Martin F. Powell

Miss Willoughby was glad that things seemed to be all right, although she *would* have liked to know exactly how much was in her Christmas Club now. Was it fifty dollars? Did the bank really put in ten dollars every month from November through March? They could have told her, couldn't they? And what did they mean by "alleviate"? Miss Willoughby looked the word up in her dictionary. It said "to make less hard to bear." What did this mean? Did she have to go on worrying about her Christmas Club all year, but less than before?

Miss Willoughby, confused, sat down and wrote another letter to the bank. . . .

I've embroidered this story a little, but the letter to Miss Willoughby (that's not her name) was actually written and sent. A copy of it is right in front of me as I write.

Why didn't the writer start with saying "Don't worry"? Why didn't he tell Miss Willoughby exactly how much was in the account? And why did he use the fancy phrase "alleviate your concern" in writing to Miss Willoughby, whose undated, hand-written note showed clearly she was a woman with little education?

Of course everybody knows the answer to the last question. People use long words in business writing because that's the way it's done. Whenever I showed this letter to my classes and said it should have started with "Don't worry," the students started an argument. "Don't worry" was too simple, they said. You can't use such words in a business letter. It sounded—well, too ordinary, too plain, too short. You *can't* say things like "Don't worry."

In this chapter I'll try to convince you that you can. More than that, you *should* use short words. Long words, like *alleviate* and a thousand others, are a curse, a special language that comes between writer and reader, a curtain that prevents them from understanding each other fully.

Why do people use so many long words in writing? I've collected a list of the most common of these long, pompous words—we'll get to that list in a minute—and I've found that the reasons are various. Some pompous words are used because the writer wants to cloak himself in a mantle of false dignity. Some are used for hedging. Some are used to convey the power of the organization that stands behind the writer or the powerlessness of the addressee.

Many pomposities are used because writers are conditioned to shy away from simple, everyday words and search for a more dignified substitute.

And some are used simply because the writer wants to show off.

The phrase "alleviate your concern" is a particularly good example because (1) the writer obviously reached for a dignified substitute for "don't worry," (2) the addressee probably didn't understand it, and (3) it doesn't mean what the writer thought it meant.

Like the lady who warned against using foreign phrases "because you never can tell what they mean," business writers who blithely use their formal vocabulary fall into some verbal trap in every second or third paragraph. They misuse *anticipate* for *expect, transpire* for *happen,* and *presently* for *now.* They use words that have unintended connotations. They bury the meaning of what they say in a fog of vague verbiage.

Well-educated, truly literate people don't write that way. Many years ago I had an idea for a book that would serve as a thesaurus of simple words for those anxious to simplify their style. I assembled a panel of twelve outstanding people—a famous editor, a widely known attorney, a prominent doctor, and so on—and had them check questionnaires with lists of long, pompous words. They were asked whether and how often they used those words in speaking or writing.

I had to abandon the project, and so I never got around to using my data. But the thing I remember most clearly is that each of those highly literate people admitted that he or she used almost all those words sometimes—but only in a humorous sense. In other words, they all might have said "alleviate your concern," but they would have said it with a smile, playing a little game with the English language. Not one of them would have used the phrase in dead seriousness while writing to Miss Willoughby.

There are thousands of these words that poison people's writing. Probably you're using a good many of them every day. How can I get you to kick the habit? I thought about this problem a great deal and finally came to the following conclusion: I'll give you a list of the most common of these words—long enough to cover those most widely used but short enough for you to remember each word individually and feel a twinge whenever you're about to put it on paper. There are sixty words on my list, and I honestly think that if I rob you of those sixty words, you'll be seriously hampered in using your accustomed pompous style.

I don't mean to say these words should be taboo on all occasions. All I want you to do is to *avoid using them as substitutes for the simple words you'd use in talking to your reader.*

Here's my list:

THE 60-WORD BLACKLIST

1. *advise* (write)
2. *affirmative* (yes)
3. *anticipate* (expect)
4. *appear* (seem)
5. *ascertain* (find out)
6. *assist* (help)
7. *complete* (fill out)
8. *comply* (follow)
9. *constitute* (be)
10. *cooperate* (help)
11. *deceased* (dead)
12. *deem* (think)
13. *desire* (want)
14. *determine* (figure, find)
15. *disclose* (show)
16. *effect* (make)
17. *elect* (choose, pick)
18. *endeavor* (try)
19. *ensue* (follow)
20. *execute* (sign)
21. *experience* (have)
22. *facilitate* (make easy)
23. *failed to* (didn't)
24. *forward* (send)
25. *furnish* (send)
26. *inasmuch as* (since)
27. *inconvenience* (trouble)
28. *indicate* (say, show)
29. *initial* (first)
30. *in lieu of* (instead of)
31. *insufficient* (not enough)
32. *in the event that* (if)
33. *locate* (find)
34. *negative* (no)
35. *obtain* (get)
36. *personnel* (people)
37. *pertaining to* (of, about)
38. *presently* (now)
39. *prior to* (before)
40. *prohibit* (forbid)
41. *provide* (give, say)
42. *pursuant to* (under)
43. *represent* (be)
44. *request* (ask for)
45. *require* (need)
46. *residence* (home, address)
47. *reveal* (show)
48. *review* (check)
49. *spouse* (wife, husband)
50. *state* (say)
51. *submit* (give, send)
52. *subsequent* (later)
53. *substantial* (big, large, great)
54. *sufficient* (enough)
55. *supply* (send)
56. *sustain* (suffer)
57. *terminate* (end, stop)
58. *thus* (so, that way)
59. *transpire* (happen)
60. *vehicle* (car, truck)

Let's look at each of these words more closely.

1. *advise.* This is the only word on the list that bears the unmistakable stamp of business writing. Dictionaries mark its use in the sense of *inform, notify, write* as strictly "commercial." Nobody ever *says* "I wish to advise"; it's the hallmark of "commercial correspondence."

Back in 1930 I was a student at the *Hochschule für Welthandel* (International Trade College) in Vienna. I took a course in English Business Writing and I still remember Herr Knoll, who was an excellent teacher, drumming into us the hallowed phrases "I beg to acknowledge receipt of your favor . . ." and "We wish to advise . . ." Herr Knoll taught us what he thought was the best English usage, but unfortunately he was even then some fifty years out of date (and of course he taught us British usage into the bargain). So the first and only course I ever took in English was in thoroughly Victorian, old-fashioned, *Forsyte Saga* "business English."

Please think of Herr Knoll whenever you feel the urge to write "Please be advised."

2. *affirmative.* I put the word *affirmative* on my list because I want to remind you of the simple, extremely useful word *yes.* It's very rare to see the word *yes* in a business letter or official document and yet it's one of the handiest words in the English language. I said before that you should use more questions with question marks at the end. Well, the next step is to use the words *yes* and *no.*

Of course, as long as you're ashamed of using the beautiful word *yes* and hide behind the cumbersome four-syllable word *affirmative,* there isn't much point in using the question-and-answer technique. So repress the urge to say "affirmative." Say "yes." Instead of "We expect the company will make an affirmative reply" say "We think they'll say yes."

And whenever you can, use my favorite opening for an answer to a complaint letter: "Yes, you're right."

3. *anticipate.* Pompous writers always use *anticipate* instead of *expect.* Why? Because *anticipate* has four syllables and *expect* only two. So *anticipate* sounds more impressive.

The trouble is that the two words don't mean the same thing. When I *expect* something, I simply think it's going to happen; but when I *anticipate* it, I act on that forecast and do something either to forestall it or to benefit from my foreknowledge. A man who *expects* rain may cast a doubtful glance at the sky but take a chance; a man who *anticipates* rain takes an umbrella. A boy and a girl who *expect* to be married look forward to their wedding day; but if they *anticipate* marriage, they go to bed together.

Of course, since bad writers for some fifty or a hundred years have used *anticipate* when they mean *expect,* the difference between the two words has been almost washed away. But not quite. *Anticipate* still means something more, something stronger. If I *anticipate* something, although I may not actually do anything to discount or prevent it, at least I have a greater sense of certainty than if I simply *expect* it. Therefore, the word *anticipate,* when used to a customer, has an air of arrogance about it. Its implied meaning is "I expect you to do such-and-such *or else."*

One of the letters in my collection ends with the words "Your prompt attention to this request for payment is *anticipated."* Do you hear the nasty undertone?

4. *appear. Appear* and *seem* are the two great hedging words. Nothing is stated as a fact; nothing is written down without an out. The timid, hedging writer lives in a world of shadowy appearances. He doesn't say there's a difference between the figures; he says "There appears to be a discrepancy." He doesn't say there's a disagreement; he says "Apparently there has been a misunderstanding."

The technique of hedging and dodging responsibility means that you never say a fact is a fact; you hide behind *appear, apparent, seems* and *seemingly* and imply you're only talking about a first-glance impression which may be wrong.

It says on your books that your customer owes you $52.60. But that only *appears* to be true; maybe a check of his has been lost in the mails, or an item has been misposted, or the computer has mixed up some numbers. Innumerable students of mine have earnestly defended their hedging; they've pointed out to me that mistakes are made all the time and you can never be sure that an apparent fact is a fact. My answer, over the years, has always been the same. Sure, there are frequent mistakes; sure, your own company or agency may be at fault; but don't always assume you're in the wrong. Instead, assume that things have gone their normal way; the mail has been delivered properly, the accounting has been in order, the computers have done their work as programmed. Why expect trouble, when you *know* that mistakes happen only in a minority of cases? Say what you have to say in the simplest possible way. The customer owes you money. The merchandise has been delivered. The signature has *not* been a forgery. If there *has* been a mistake and someone in your own company has blundered, you'll hear about it soon enough. Don't try to protect yourself with these silly *apparently*s and *seemingly*s; legally they're not worth a damn anyway.

(The business with the signature that may just possibly have been forged reminds me of the standard banking phrase for saying that a signature looks genuine. They never say so in so many words; they say "It conforms favorably with the one in our files.")

So don't start a letter with "We appear to be without response to our letter of . . ." Ten to one—a hundred to one—a thousand to one—they just didn't answer.

5. *ascertain.* A poor writer never says "find out"; he always makes it "ascertain." A nice, fancy word—a word he never uses in speaking, so it must be really elegant and refined. Don't do it. When you mean "find out," say "find out."

Newspaper reporters in particular hate to admit they don't know or haven't been able to find out. I quote from a recent story in the *New York Times:* "The meeting is also understood to have considered a new format for the *Saturday Review* that would emphasize a different topic in each issue, although it could not be immediately *ascertained* whether Mr. Cousins and the new owner reached agreement over this question." What the reporter meant was that he tried to find out but couldn't.

6. *assist.* A sales clerk in a store says "May I help you?" But a correspondent in a letter writes "We are glad to be of assistance." *Help* is too ordinary a word; the business writer uses *assist* and *assistance* to decorate his pages.

Sometimes the word *assist* sounds downright silly, as in "Enclosed is a self-addressed envelope which will *assist* you in returning the statement."

And sometimes *assistance* has a threatening undertone, as in "We ask your *assistance* in not drawing checks unless you are certain your bank balance is sufficient to cover them."

7. *complete.* People are never asked to fill out forms; they're always asked to *complete* them. This is particularly bad, since I'd estimate that the majority of the American population doesn't know the meaning of the word *complete* in the sense of filling out a form. They certainly never use it in that sense; and they'd be surprised if someone explained to them the idea that a form is incomplete as long as they don't put in the required information in pencil or ink. So the ordinary person, when asked to "complete" a form, always has to adjust his mind to the fact that this means "fill it out."

But of course by now everybody has filled out so many forms that they do it automatically as soon as they see the boxes and the dotted lines.

8. *comply.* I looked up *comply* in the dictionary and found, to my surprise, that it stems from the same root as *complete.* It literally means "to fill out or fulfill." The law says something should be done, and the citizen fulfills his duty and does his part by *complying.* It's a very strong word. If you say "Comply with the rules," there's a threat of enforcement behind it; if you say "Follow the rules," it means the same thing, but it's gentler and nicer.

Comply is a word for laws and official rules, but if it's used by a business firm or private organization ("We hope you will comply with our request"), it's arrogant.

9. *constitute.* The dictionary definition of *constitute* is *form, make* or *make up,* but most people use it simply as a fancy synonym for *be.*

A newspaper story says: "The actions *constitute* a significant departure in government pollution control efforts, which until now have relied on civil actions." Why not "The actions *are* . . ."? The writer probably thought there was a subtle difference in meaning, but if you look closely you'll find that *are* says exactly the same thing here as *constitute*.

Don't use the ten-letter word *constitute*. Say *is* or *are*.

10. *cooperate*. Of course *cooperate* and *cooperation* are perfectly good words. They're even beautiful in their connotations. But the way they're used nowadays in official and business writing is a mockery of their great and glorious past.

The typical letter writer never gives any thought to cooperating with his addressee, but he certainly wants the other fellow to cooperate with *him*. "Cooperate with the inevitable" is his motto—in other words, "Do as I say." And so he writes "Thank you in advance for your cooperation"—meaning you'd better pay our bill or fill out our questionnaire or whatever it is we want you to do.

"We sincerely hope that we may have your cooperation in the future conduct of your account," a bank writes—meaning "No more overdrafts, or else."

Don't use *cooperate* and *cooperation* whenever you mean "Do what you're told." At the least, it'll strike your reader as a phony word; but it may also antagonize him and have the opposite effect from the one you're after.

11. *deceased*. As you know, this is the word used in official or business documents to refer to someone who died. You may say "What's wrong with using a euphemism?" but you'd be wrong. *Deceased* is *not* a euphemism for *dead*. A euphemism is a more pleasant word used instead of one that has unpleasant connotations. In talking of someone who died, people often use the euphemism *passed away;* but they never say *deceased*. Can you say to a recent widow "I was so sorry to hear your husband is deceased"? You can't.

If you look in Webster's Unabridged Dictionary, you'll find the word *dysphemism,* meaning "substitution of a disagreeable, offen-

sive, or disparaging word or expression for an agreeable or in-
offensive one (as . . . *old man* for *father,* or *heap* for *car*)." By
that definition, *deceased* is a dysphemism. So, by the way, are the
other fifty-nine words on my list. It's a list of dysphemisms.

What should you use instead of *deceased?* It depends. Most often,
you'd naturally use the name of the person who died. For instance,
the sentence "The lump-sum death benefits were paid in accordance
with an authorization from Mrs. Mary Bowers, daughter of the *deceased* wage earner" should have been written ". . . from Mrs. Mary
Bowers, Mr. Porter's daughter."

Sometimes a simple pronoun will do. A form letter used by the
Social Security Administration starts: "Our records show that survivors' benefits on the account of the above cannot be paid since *the
deceased* did not have enough social security credit." This is a letter
people get shortly after the death of their father or mother. Why add
to their grief by using the ruthlessly cold word *deceased?* It would have
been just as clear to write ". . . since he (she) didn't have enough
social security credit."

12. *deem.* This is a very formal and legal word, meaning *consider*
or *think.* Actually it means more than either of those words. If you
deem something, you judge it to be as you say, and your *deeming*
makes it so, because you're in a position of power. When the Social
Security Administration writes to an applicant "We *deem* your letter
to be a request for reconsideration," they mean "You didn't use the
right words in your letter, but we'll consider it a proper legal appeal
anyway. Since it's up to us to say so, that's what it is."

Just the other day, I found an excellent example of this dictatorial
use of the word *deem* in a sample contract for a photographer's model.
It said "I hereby give and grant (to the Company) the absolute and
unconditional right to use pictures of me . . . for art, advertising,
trademark, trade or any lawful purpose whatever, all as the Company, in its absolute discretion, shall *deem* fit."

You see? *Deem* is a word that naturally lends itself to tying someone up hand and foot. Don't use it in ordinary writing. On second

thought, don't even use it in legal documents. It sounds too nasty. *Think* or *consider* will serve the purpose just as well.

13. *desire.* In everyday speech, if you like, care for or prefer something, you use the word *want.* But in writing, you shy away from it. Too ordinary. You go up one notch on the scale of formality or pomposity and you say *wish.* But since people have done so for so long a time, *wish* by now isn't good enough either. So you use *desire*—a word that means *longing, craving* or *lust*—to express any slight preference.

"Please indicate whether you *desire* a regular or special account." . . . "If it is *desired,* we shall proceed with legal action." . . . "If you so *desire,* we shall give you footnote credit." What a comedown for a word meaning deep longing or hot passion!

Don't use *desire* when you mean *want.* Don't even use *wish.* Don't degrade these deeply emotional words by using them for your dull, drab business purposes.

14. *determine. Determine* and *determination* are long words beloved by pompous writers, because they can be used instead of the brief, simple English words *find, find out, figure, figure out, fix, set, test* and *decide.* Pick whatever word fits your sentence, but *don't* use *determine.* It's like weighing down your sentence with lead.

Here's a prize example: "After an extensive investigation of our files, we have *determined* that the material relating to this apparent duplication is at the disposal of our Adjustment Section." What does this mean? It means "We've found your file in the adjustment section."

15. *disclose.* I put the word *disclose* on my blacklist because business and official writers have a habit of making a tremendous production out of the simple phrase "our records show." They never just *show;* they *disclose* or *reveal.* Don't play these silly games with your reader. Don't pretend you were utterly amazed and dumbfounded when you discovered he owes your company $10.50.

16. *effect.* The word *effect* can be used with splendid results to change a simple word into a phrase at least four times longer and more impressive-looking. Instead of *paid* you write *effected payment;*

instead of *deliver* you write *effect delivery*. Nothing easier than that. Guaranteed to make your sentences slow as molasses.

17. *elect*. When ordinary people think of elections, they think of the first Tuesday after the first Monday in November. But in official language the word *elect* is regularly used where everybody else would say *choose* or *pick*—or leave the choice to the reader by using the simple word *or*. "Under the terms of your agreement, you may *elect* to pay the loan in full at this time, or make partial payments during the grace period." Why make it sound so complicated? Say "Your agreement says you can pay off your loan now or in installments during the grace period."

18. *endeavor*. Another one of those words used just to make things heavier and longer. The regular word is *try*.

Rewrite a sentence like "If the drawees have not yet complied with the terms of the draft, please *endeavor* to ascertain their reasons for not doing so." Change it to "If the draft hasn't been paid, please *try* to find out why."

19. *ensue*. The word *ensue* means that something happens as a result or consequence of something else. Don't—*please don't*—use it to express the simple passage of time; for that we have the word *follow*.

Nobody uses the word *ensue* in talking; it's strictly a paper word. "In the *ensuing* twelve months, Hughes Tool has won a series of court tests." Nonsense. The twelve months didn't *ensue* as a result of what happened to the Hughes Tool company; they just passed by— spring, summer, fall and winter.

20. *execute*. An execution, to you and me, means the electric chair, the gallows or a firing squad. But to the official mind it means the peaceful act of signing a piece of paper.

"A Xerox copy of the form is enclosed for execution." Don't get frightened. It just means you're supposed to sign it.

Have I cured you of the habit of using *execute* for *sign*? I hope so.

21. *experience*. If you can't find a piece of paper, how can you make it sound as if you'd put a great deal of time and effort into the

search but were frustrated by circumstances beyond your control? Simple: You write "We regret to inform you that we are *experiencing* difficulties in locating this item and would appreciate your favoring us with a copy of same."

"Experience," says the dictionary, is "practical wisdom resulting from what one has encountered, undergone, or lived through." What kind of wisdom do you get from not finding a piece of paper in the files? Ask yourself that question before you write "We are experiencing difficulties in locating this item."

22. *facilitate*. Don't write *facilitate* when you mean *make easy*. Don't be guilty of sentences like "To *facilitate* the submission of this statement we are enclosing a self-addressed envelope."

23. *failed to, failure*. To illustrate my point about the words *failed to* and *failure*, I'll quote a recent item from a New York newspaper:

> Mrs. Charles Phillips, who is 82 years old and sick, was evicted yesterday from her home in Tudor City.
> She had lived in a six-room apartment at the Essex House, 325 East 41st Street, since her husband's death in 1940, but she had to be put out, the landlord said, for *failure* to pay two months' rent.

The story went on to tell about how Mrs. Phillips' precious furniture, china and glassware were carried out to the sidewalk and how the police tried to take her away in an ambulance. Her monthly rent was $169. Her niece, who attended to her affairs, had arranged to get the $338 for two months' rent by selling some securities, but the landlord had been too quick in getting an eviction order so he could rent the apartment to a new tenant for over $300 a month.

And so poor old Mrs. Phillips was forcefully put out of her rent-controlled apartment. Her "failure" to pay the rent consisted simply in her niece being a little careless about paying bills.

I wanted to tell this pitiful story because people nowadays always write of *failing* and *failure* when they simply mean that someone didn't do something. Well, the words don't mean just that. They carry a clear overtone of guilt. When I write "You *failed* to answer my letter," I imply that you *should* have answered it and were negligent. When I write of "your *failure* to pay this invoice," I'm really saying you fell down on your obligations and are sloppy and careless in conducting your affairs.

Who knows whether that's true? Doesn't our legal system say people should be considered innocent until proven guilty? Mrs. Phillips wasn't guilty of anything; she was just an unhappy victim of circumstances. Don't accuse people of their *failure* to do what you want them to do. Give them the benefit of doubt. "Sorry we didn't hear from you" is much, much better than "You failed to respond."

Anyway, you never use the word *failure* when you're writing about yourself, do you? You don't say "We *failed* to find your letter." Oh, no. You yourself are always blameless. So you write "We regret to inform you that we experienced difficulties in locating this item."

Come on. Be fair. Don't use *fail* and *failure* to accuse people of wrongdoing.

24. *forward.* "We will *forward* our check . . . itemized bills . . . checkbooks and deposit slips . . . full and detailed information." Why do business writers always *forward* pieces of paper instead of simply *sending* them? Obviously because *forward* is a heavier, heftier, more pompous word than *send.* When you say *forward,* it sounds like shipping something heavy and important, like ball bearings or lumber or farm machinery. When you *forward* a simple, featherweight piece of paper, you clothe it with ponderous significance.

I think I'll allow you to use the word *forward* for checks for over $100,000. Otherwise, say *send.*

25. *furnish.* When business writers don't *forward* pieces of paper, they *furnish* them. What's usually furnished in business letters is "a complete report . . . the requested information . . . booklets and check stuffers." Again, the word *furnish* sounds like much more than these light items. The dictionary defines *furnish* as "to provide or supply with what is needed, useful or desirable" and mentions "furniture and appliances."

When you're sending someone a couple of measly leaflets, don't say you're *furnishing* them. Just *send* them along without making a big fuss.

26. *inasmuch as.* I put *inasmuch as* on my list because it's one of the best examples of an unnecessary compound conjunction. There's no context I know of where *since* wouldn't be better than *inasmuch as.*

The basic principle is, Avoid all prepositions and conjunctions that consist of more than one word. Aside from *inasmuch as,* this includes *with regard to, in association with, in connection with, with respect to, in the absence of, with a view to, in an effort to, in terms of, in order to, for the purpose of, for the reason that, in accordance with, in the neighborhood of, on the basis of,* and so on. There's not a single one of these word combinations that can't be replaced by a simple word like *if, for, to, by, about* or *since.*

Pruning your style of these cumbersome expressions is good exercise for you. If you're an *inasmuch as* addict, start right there.

27. *inconvenience.* When your company or organization has made a mistake and someone complains, you write a letter of apology and say you regret the *inconvenience.*

Do you know what the word *inconvenience* means? I'm afraid you don't. Let me quote from *Webster's Dictionary of Synonyms:* "*Inconvenience* usually suggests little more than interference with one's plans, one's comfort, one's freedom, or the like: it seldom carries suggestions of more than a temporary or slight disturbance or annoyance; as, I hope the new arrangement will not *inconvenience* you; do not *inconvenience* him by intruding upon him while he is writing; will it *inconvenience* you to send an answer by return mail?"

As you see, an *inconvenience* is something slight and minor. Why is it then that the word is used in *all* business letters of apology, regardless of what the customer or client went through? He may have lost hundreds of dollars or months of valuable time, he may have suffered sheer agony of frustration. Never mind, you apologize to him for the *inconvenience* caused. What happens to your own company or organization is always taken with the utmost seriousness and solemnity; but what happens to others, *even if it's your fault,* is never more than an *inconvenience*—just a slight spot of bother, hardly worth mentioning.

I've always felt that if I taught my students to drop the word *inconvenience* forever from their vocabulary—or at least from their letter-of-apology vocabulary—they got their money's worth out of my course. There's nothing quite as thoughtless and callous as the standard American use of the word *inconvenience.*

And now let me tell you a story.

For many years my wife and I have exchanged Christmas presents with our old friends Mr. and Mrs. McGregor (that's not their real name). Last November we picked an unusual item—a certain monthly magazine we knew they'd like to read. So we sent our check and entered a subscription for them.

Christmas came and our present from the McGregors arrived in good time, but all they got from us was a little card saying that a Christmas gift subscription to such-and-such a magazine had been entered for them by the Flesches. A month or two went by and sometime in February or March the McGregors, with much embarrassment, told us they'd never got the magazine.

I got on the phone immediately. A lady took down all the particulars and said she'd attend to the matter right away. She did too—after just a few weeks the McGregors got another little Christmas card telling them the Flesches had subscribed for them to such-and-such a magazine. But of the magazine itself there wasn't a trace.

Naturally it's highly embarrassing to tell your friends that their promised gifts haven't arrived. But eventually—after a couple more months had gone by—the McGregors felt they had to tell us. This time I was really furious. I wrote the magazine what I thought was a very strongly worded letter, pointing out that they'd cashed my check way back in November and asking them in no uncertain terms to start sending the magazine—with all the copies missed since Christmas—*instantly.*

There was no answer whatever. Another month passed, and after unhappily checking with the McGregors, I wrote another letter and sent a copy to the Better Business Bureau.

That did it. On August 4 the company wrote they were entering a new subscription for the McGregors, beginning with the September issue.

And how did they start their letter after nine months of intense embarrassment and aggravation? You guessed it: "Please accept our sincerest apologies for any *inconvenience* you have encountered with your gift subscription."

7   *Use Short Words* (2)

I'll go on with my blacklist.

28. *indicate, indication.* When I asked my twelve-year-old daughter Janet what was the meaning of the word *indicate,* she immediately came back with "To indicate means to give you an idea of something."

She was perfectly right. To *indicate* means to hint, to suggest, to point toward something indirectly without actually saying so in so many words.

You'd think that if Janet knows that, everyone would know, but that isn't so at all. *Indicate* is used by business and official writers in almost every other paragraph, meaning *say, show, write down, express precisely.* They've completely lost the feeling for the indirect, tentative nature of what's *indicated* rather than actually *said* or *shown.* To them, the words mean the same thing.

In a lawyer's letter I found this sentence: "It is our intention to proceed with suit by an attachment of the debtor's bank account and upon receipt of our requirements we will immediately proceed *as indicated.*" What did he mean by *as indicated?* Answer: He meant what he'd just said in so many words. What he should have written was ". . . we'll do so immediately."

In an ad by a book club that offers four books for one dollar, with

a list of titles to pick from, I found four boxes in the coupon, preceded by the words *"Indicate* by number the four books you want."
What does *indicate* mean here? Obviously it means "write in." There's no other way of indicating a number than by putting down "461" or "234." Possibly one might indicate "1776" by drawing a picture of an American flag, but I don't think that's what the copywriter had in mind.

So please don't use *indicate.* I know, it's a beautiful combination pomposity and hedge word, but try to restrain yourself. As I said before, hedging really doesn't do any good. When you write someone "Our records *indicate* that you are in arrears with your payments," you've dunned him. Don't kid yourself. Don't pretend you can hide behind the word *indicate* if it turns out he's paid his bill on the dot.

29. *initial.* "Upon receipt of your *initial deposit* . . . We have reversed our *initial* decision . . . You will receive the *initial* volume . . ." I've never seen a business or official letter where the word *initial* couldn't be replaced by *first.* Sheer pomposity, love of long words, false dignity, urge to show off, or whatever. Don't use *initial.*

30. *in lieu of.* Have you ever heard anyone say *in lieu of* in conversation? Of course not. It's strictly a legal-document, police-blotter kind of word. In ordinary writing it should be utterly taboo.

I was amused when I found a neat specimen of *in lieu of* in a full-page ad for coffee in a popular magazine. The company offered a contest, with an original portrait by Norman Rockwell as the first prize. "If Norman Rockwell is unable to complete the portrait," the ad said, "a cash award of $20,000 will be made *in lieu thereof.*" In my mind I could see the copywriter tearing his hair about that unsightly phrase in his slick folksy copy and the guy from the legal department insisting that "in lieu thereof" was absolutely necessary or the ad would have to be withdrawn.

31. *insufficient. Insufficient* means *not enough,* and that's really all that needs to be said. The rest is up to you. Go through your writing and replace every *insufficient* by *not enough.* Result: You've improved your style.

32. *in the event that. If* has one syllable and two letters; *in the event that* has five syllables and fourteen letters. Which is why stiff, pompous, overformal writers studiously avoid the little word *if* and use *in the event that* with monotonous regularity.

Here again is a simple improvement you can make with hardly any effort. Whenever you've written *in the event that*—or are about to write it—say *if*. Which is easy, except for the fact that it'll probably take you years to make it an invariable habit. Well, you just have to work at it. It's worth it, I assure you.

33. *locate.* When you *find* something that was lost, you have a certain feeling of triumph, but when you just *locate* it, it's sort of blah. However, some business writers never say *find*. They always *locate*. "We regret that due to unavoidable circumstances, we are unable to *locate* these entries on microfilm. . . ." They didn't try very hard to *find* them, did they?

34. *negative.* Don't say *negative,* say *no*. "We regret to report that we received a *negative* reply." What you mean is, "Sorry, but they said *no."* And there it is, crystal clear and unmistakable.

Incidentally, write it "They said no." Don't put quotation marks around *no* and make it "They said 'No.'" Actually, they didn't use the actual word *no* in their answer; what they said was something like "We quite appreciate your point of view, but what with our present tight budget and all the uncertainties in the economy, we feel we owe it to our stockholders to cut down on expenditures right now." So don't use quotation marks around words that were never uttered or written.

35. *obtain.* Untrained writers are always unreasonably afraid of using the word *get*. *Get* is just about the most commonly used verb in current English, so they shrink away from it as if it were useless and utterly, utterly vulgar. Well, if you want to learn how to write, get used to the word *get*. It's incredibly useful.

"You may *obtain* more detailed information . . ." Hold it right there. Cross out every single *obtain*. And while you're at it, cross out *procure, secure* and, in most places, *receive*. *Get* is always better. It's the way we all talk. Got it?

36. *personnel.* Need I say anything about *personnel?* We live in the age of "antipersonnel weapons," which are defined in Webster's Unabridged Dictionary as weapons "designed to destroy, maim, or obstruct military personnel." If they were called "anti-people" weapons, maybe world disarmament would come a little sooner.

37. *pertain.* This is one of the most unnecessary words in the language. *Pertain* or *pertaining to* can always be replaced by a simple *of, on* or *about.* "Here is the information *pertaining to* the present case" means "Here's the information on this case." That's all. *Pertain* has no meaning. It's just a part of the language inflation that's going on.

38. *presently.* Several hundred years ago, *presently* was used to mean *now,* but its current dictionary meaning is *soon.* So, just to confuse things, business writers always say *presently* when they mean *now,* on the general principle of Why use a short word when I can use a longer one?

Resist the temptation. Say *now* when you mean *now.*

39. *prior to.* I admit I've heard people use *prior to* in conversation. Is the good old word *before* really going to disappear from the language?

I still have hopes. At least, I'll certainly do the best I can to talk you into using the word *before* instead of the insidious *prior to.* It just isn't the same thing. Do you watch TV *before* you go to bed? Or do you watch it *prior to* going to bed? Ah, come off it.

And don't think you can escape into *preliminary to, preparatory to* or *previous to.* They're much worse. You can see that, can't you?

40. *prohibit. Prohibit* to me always sounds like *Verboten!* in Nazi Germany. At least say *forbid.* It sounds a little less like a police state.

41. *provide.* It always sounds more pompous and official if you *provide* something, instead of just *saying, giving, sending, setting* or *fixing* it. Here are some choice examples:

"The Social Security Act *provides* that the amount of a worker's benefit shall be based on his average monthly earnings." Cut it out. Say the law *says* so.

"We shall be obliged if you could *provide us with* photocopies of the items in question." Rewrite. "Please send us copies of these items."

"Hoping the afore-going information will *provide* temporary satisfaction, we remain." This one really defies translation into decent English. Let's skip it and start all over from scratch. Let's write "Please bear with us meanwhile."

And now a sentence with *two provides* in it: "The compromise further *provided* relatively modest fees for *providing* day care to children of families earning more than $4,320." Which means: "The compromise further *fixed* (or *set*) relatively modest fees for *giving* day care to children in families earning more than $4,320."

42. *pursuant to.* This, of course, is very common in legal writing, where it simply means *under.* "*Pursuant to* Regulation Z" means "*Under* Regulation Z."

What really gags me is to see *pursuant to* creeping into the ordinary language. "*Pursuant to* our telephone conversation this morning, we are enclosing a preliminary brochure . . ." All this means is "Here's the brochure I said I'd send you."

43. *represent.* This word, like *constitute,* is often misused as a resounding three-syllable substitute for *is* or *are.* "The purchase of the Granville property *represented* our largest transaction during the fiscal year." Why not *was?* Nobody knows. Somehow it never *is*—it *represents,* it *constitutes,* and if it's on the company's books, it *reflects.*

44. *request.* A *request* means more than just *asking* for something. It's a demand for something that's due. Don't misuse the word *request.* Say it more nicely. A little courtesy and politeness won't do any harm.

45. *require.* I've never found an instance where the word *require* couldn't be replaced by *need.* The two words mean exactly the same. Why say *require?* I don't see the need.

46. *residence.* "A house of superior or pretentious character," Webster says. The word makes me think of marble pillars and stately porticoes and an air of grandeur, like governors' residences in eighteenth-century colonies or the enormous palatial *Residenz* of the prince-archbishops in the lovely city of Salzburg.

But in twentieth-century American business writing the beautiful word *residence* has fallen on evil days. It means *house* or *home* and sometimes it means even less than that. In the sentence "If you rent a *residence,* our tenant's policy is designed especially for you," it means just an apartment; in the sentence "We have verified the debtor's *residence,*" it merely means an address.

47. *reveal.* If you don't *disclose,* you *reveal.* The records never simply *show.* We looked at your account and—surprise, surprise!—it *revealed* that you still owe us six dollars for dog food.

48. *review.* Another grand word. Webster's mentions "an inspection of troops under arms, followed by their marching past a high officer." It also mentions "passing one's life in review." It does *not* mention "A review of our records indicates . . ."

Stop all this posturing. Say "We found."

49. *spouse.* Surely there's nobody who doesn't realize this is a funny word. It belongs to stand-up comedians rather than the rest of us. And yet, legal and not-so-legal documents are filled with *spouses* instead of *husbands* and *wives,* without anybody laughing out loud.

This morning, for instance, I saw a newspaper ad by a men's store asking people to volunteer as blood donors. "When you give blood," the ad said, "you receive an unlimited blood replacement credit for yourself, *spouse* and children for a whole year." Why use the ugly word *spouse?* Because it would have been a little awkward to write "for yourself, your wife or husband and your children"? The way I look at it, *anything* is better than *spouse.*

50. *state.* A police-blotter word, beloved by all bureaucrats. "Mr. French *stated* he was dissatisfied with the decision. . . ." No, he didn't just *state* it. In fact, he came to the office and said so with great noise and excitement.

If everything said is just a *statement,* you've taken all the drama out of human life.

51. *submit.* Business writers don't realize that *submit* has to do with *submission,* that is, buckling under and yielding to superior force. Why use a word with such unpleasant connotations?

"At your earliest convenience please *submit* photostatic copies of the actual checks. . . ." Don't. Say "Please *send* us as soon as possible . . ." Don't treat a fellow citizen like a humble supplicant or a beggar at the gate.

52. *subsequent, subsequently. Prior to* instead of *before* is bad enough, but *subsequent to* instead of *after* is worse. Why people insist on using this hippopotamus of a word escapes me. It's ugly, it's cumbersome, it has no advantages whatever over *after* or *later,* and yet everything I read about happened *subsequent to* something else.

The other day I read this sentence in a newspaper: "The commission has insufficient evidence at the present time that Zerex, as reformulated *subsequent to* that initial marketing of the product, is capable of causing damage to automotive cooling systems." One bureaucratic monster word piled upon another, and another, and another. Let me translate: "The commission hasn't enough evidence now that Zerex, as reformulated *after* its first marketing, can cause damage to automotive cooling systems." Lets in some daylight, doesn't it?

53. *substantial.* It is rare nowadays to find the words *large, big, much, great* and *heavy* in a business letter or official document. Everything is *substantial.* It's never "a *large* amount," it's always "a *substantial* amount." It's never *"much* improved," it's always *"substantially* improved." It's never "a *big* increase," it's always "a *substantial* increase."

There's no reason for this, except the bureaucrat's love of long words. If you think that *substantial* is somehow more precise or definite than *big, large* or *great,* you're very much mistaken. One dictionary definition, for instance, says *substantial* means "considerable, ample, large." Another one says "important." A third says "of moment." And so it goes.

Legal definitions aren't any better. Under the social security law, for example, you can't get disability insurance if you're able to perform a "substantial gainful activity." And what is a substantial gainful activity? The official "Social Security Handbook" defines it like this: "The term 'substantial gainful activity' used to describe the level of work activity means work activity that is both substantial and gainful. Substantial work activity involves the performance of significant physical or mental duties, or a combination of both, productive in nature . . . In order for work activity to be substantial, it is not necessary that it be performed on a full-time basis; work activity performed on a part-time basis may also be substantial." *Now* do you know what *substantial* means?

Recently I got an advertising letter from an automobile insurance company. It said: "You may save a *substantial* amount of cash on your automobile insurance . . . Savings of $10, $30, even as much as $50 a year may be yours." Quite a spread, isn't it?

And in a magazine article I came across a warning against "future problems *of substantial magnitude.*" Wow!

54. *sufficient*. The word *sufficient* means exactly the same as *enough*. There's simply no excuse for using the longer, more cumbersome word.

55. *supply*. Another mouthful of a word. *Supply*, like *furnish* or *forward*, sounds big and bulky. It also has connotations of "long-lasting," like, for instance, a year's *supply* of groceries.

But of course in business and government what is usually supplied are pieces of paper. Letter writers *supply* forms, Xerox copies and envelope stuffers. Sometimes they go a little further and *supply* leaflets.

Instead of *supply*, say *send*.

56. *sustain*. Why is it that someone else's injuries are always *sustained?* I think it's because when we're *sustaining* something, we bear up under it, grit our teeth and endure it stoically. We don't just suffer, but accept what's happening to us with equanimity.

There's an unwritten law in business writing that says whatever happens to someone else is minor and easy to bear, but what happens to yourself is a heavy burden and causes severe damage and harm. Therefore someone else's troubles are always just *inconveniences* and his injuries are always *sustained*.

Don't be callous. Sympathize with those who *suffer* and are in *trouble*.

57. *terminate.* In business and official writing, nothing ever *ends* or *stops,* but everything *terminates* or, better still, is passively *terminated.* "Your entitlement *was terminated* effective November 1968 due to Paul's attainment of age 18 in that month." Why not "We had to *stop* your payments"? No reason. *Terminate* is simply longer and more official-sounding. *Was terminated,* in the passive voice, sounds even more final and devastating. In a letter to a widow who'd asked why her social security checks stopped coming, it sounds downright cruel.

58. *thus.* The Oxford English Dictionary calls the word *thus* "now chiefly literary or formal." If you use the word in your writing, you've clearly stamped it as formal. It's a word *nobody* uses in conversation. If you want to kill any trace of informality in your writing, use *thus*.

Instead of *thus,* use *so, that way, therefore* or *for instance.* Often the best thing to do with *thus* is to simply cross it out. Take for instance this sentence from a newspaper story on a pornography case: "He also maintained that Mr. Pomerantz, who admitted in testimony that he had sold the book, was not knowledgeable about its contents and was *thus* not responsible for them." This could just as well read: ". . . was not knowledgeable about its contents and not responsible for them." The *thus* added practically nothing to the meaning; it just made the sentence more fussy and pedantic.

59. *transpire.* This is the police-blotter synonym for *happen.* Actually, to *transpire* means to get known to the world. If something happens behind closed doors and information leaks to the outside, then it has *transpired*.

Bad writers have long forgotten that distinction, if they ever knew it, and blithely use *transpire* as a more impressive synonym for *happen*.

Once I actually found an example where someone wrote that something *transpired* that *didn't* get known: "What *transpired* at these meetings has been shrouded in unusual secrecy."

60. *vehicle.* Another police-blotter word. This one is used on the principle that if you can't find a more impressive synonym for a word, use a word that means the thing you're talking about, plus something else. So, instead of the word *car,* you use the word *vehicle,* which can mean not only *car* but also *truck* or *motorbike.* (On the same principle, you refer to a dress as a "garment," a dog as an "animal," and children as "offspring.")

If you owned a Cadillac or Rolls-Royce, you'd feel insulted if someone called your car a "vehicle." For that matter, you would— or should—feel equally insulted if you drive a Volkswagen or a Toyota.

And that ends my blacklist. Mind you, I don't mean to say you should *never* use these words. They do have their uses, most of them, in their proper places. For instance, there's nothing wrong with using the word *vehicles* when you're writing about cars *and* trucks. And I'll allow you the word *reveal* whenever you write about something that really *was* a secret until it was made known. But otherwise, don't use these sixty words. Check the impulse to reach for the more "dignified," more "impressive" synonym. Every single *thus* or *deem* or *obtain* will leave an ugly stain on your writing.

I've kept my list to sixty words because I thought that's a number you can probably cope with. Of course there are many more of those pompous synonyms—dysphemisms, if you remember—that you should avoid. Don't write about time that has *elapsed;* let it *pass.* Don't say *commence* when you mean *begin* or *start.* Don't always write *appropriate* when *proper* will do just as well. Don't use *eliminate* instead of *drop, cut* or *end.* Don't call someone an *individual;* he has a right to be called a *person,* a *man* or a *woman.*

Don't say *designate* when you mean *name.* Don't use *purchase* for *buy.* Don't write *compensation* when you mean *pay.* And don't stretch the simple verb *use* into the ugly seven-letter word *utilize.*

I'll stop here. But I hope you'll go on, spotting pompous synonyms you use in your writing and replacing them with the simple words you use in talking. Eventually you'll get to a stage when there'll be no difference between your speaking and writing vocabulary—except perhaps for certain fancy expressions you use humorously in conversation but wouldn't dream of using seriously on paper. When that time comes, you'll have really mastered the vocabulary of your own language.

Let me end this chapter with a little collection of popular phrases and sayings—the way they would appear in a business letter or official publication.

THE POOR WRITER'S ALMANACK

Initially, God created the heaven and the earth.
Do it presently!
Seek and ye shall locate.
Come and obtain it!
God assists those who assist themselves.
Man is born unto inconvenience, as the sparks fly upward.
In the event that initially you fail to succeed, endeavor, endeavor, endeavor again.
A rose by any other designation would smell as sweet.
Residence, sweet residence.
And they lived happily ever subsequently.
Furnish us this day our daily bread.
All's well that terminates well.
Sufficient and to spare.
Deceased as a doornail.

8 *React!*

Last spring, during my term as consultant for the Social Security Administration, I spent a memorable day at one of their district offices. I wanted to learn something about their routine letter writing problems and sat for several hours beside the desks of half a dozen service representatives, watching them and listening while they answered inquiries.

I was greatly impressed by their work. They were not only invariably patient and courteous, they were warm and friendly. They leaned over backward to respect the inquirers' feelings.

I remember one of them listening with extraordinary patience while an old man tried to explain the complications of his case. Finally the representative made a notation in the file and promised to take the matter up with the payment center. Immediately afterward he was confronted by a cranky old woman who complained that her case had been mishandled. He calmed her down and then discovered she'd forgotten to bring the all-important letter that contained the necessary data. Patiently he told her how the matter could be straightened out.

Behind another desk there was a cheerful middle-aged woman. She was faced by a retired businessman who just came in to ask a simple question. She answered it quickly and courteously and the man left satisfied.

At a third desk, a young girl was trying to help an elderly widow whose check had been delayed. The widow broke into tears several times during the interview, and went into rambling stories about her late husband and her various ailments. The young social security worker said she'd keep her file on hand, took down the widow's telephone number to call her when she had some news, and comforted her with amazing success. The widow left with tears of gratitude in her eyes, telling the girl over and over she was a dear.

Later that day I talked to other people in the office who had the job of answering letters. Naturally, the letters were not as warm and human as the personal interviews. How could they be? A letter is only a pale imitation of a direct personal contact.

However, on the whole I found that the Social Security Administration was—and is—remarkably good at letter writing. They work on it. They review letters periodically and constantly try to improve their tone and quality.

Here are some samples of their work.

A woman wrote in:

> You will be surprised to hear from me so soon after you thought you had me all settled and retired for good.
>
> About two or three days after my "final retirement" at the University, I had a call from Hal's Flower Shop wanting me to go to work for them . . .

The answer started like this:

> Yes, we were surprised to hear that your "retirement" lasted only a few days. Your new job sounds interesting and we're sure you'll enjoy it. We have notified our payment center that you are working again so no social security benefits will be sent to you until you let us know that your employment has terminated.

[I wouldn't have used the word *terminated,* but what does that matter as long as the spirit is right?]

Another woman sent a letter for her missing husband to the Social Security Administration. She got the following answer:

> We are sorry that we cannot help you by forwarding the enclosed letter to your husband, Mr. Grumbach.
>
> We can understand your desire to get in touch with your husband and realize that you are anxious to obtain information about him. Unfortunately, we can be of no help to you in forwarding the enclosed letter as we have no record of any address at which your husband could possibly be contacted.

[Again I'd have changed *obtain* to *get* and *contacted* to *reached,* but the tone of the letter is just right.]

A third woman had entered a contest for a five-thousand-dollar prize. She didn't really expect to win, but wondered whether this might affect her social security payments. The district office wrote back:

> As you say, the improbable is possible. You need not worry, however, about winnings from a Cashword Puzzle as they are neither wages nor earnings from self-employment and, consequently, would not affect your social security benefits. Good luck!

These are fine examples of letters with just the right touch. Over the years I've found that this is by far the most important thing about letter writing—vastly more important than grammar, spelling or vocabulary. After all, even in a huge corporation, your letter will finally land on the desk of a person—someone with feelings and emotional responses. Consciously or unconsciously, he'll respond to what he reads between the lines. He'll be annoyed if your letter is cold, he'll be pleased if you're courteous or friendly, and he'll be uneasy if he can't quite make out your attitude.

What goes for a letter addressed to an organization goes of course ten times as much for a letter addressed to a person. It's terribly easy to hit the wrong note, and most public and private organizations do it every day a thousand times.

So this chapter, dealing with the emotional aspects of a business letter, is perhaps the most important in the book.

After studying the matter for some thirty years, I've come up with a list of ten basic principles. Here they are:

THE TEN BASIC PRINCIPLES

1. Answer promptly.
2. Show you're interested.
3. Don't be too short.
4. If it's bad news, say you're sorry.
5. If it's good news, say you're glad.
6. Give everyone the benefit of doubt.
7. Never send off an angry letter.
8. Watch out for cranks.
9. Appreciate humor.
10. Be careful with form letters.

I'll take up these points one by one.

Principle No. 1. *Answer promptly.* This has nothing to do with writing as such, but of course it's tremendously important. There's nothing good to be said about delay. Try to answer every letter the same day, the next day, the third day. Don't let them sit on your desk; they'll be a load on your spirit.

Counsel of perfection, I know. But it's the Number One secret of writing good letters. Not only will your letter get less effective with each day that goes by, it'll also lose more and more of its freshness and immediacy. It's almost impossible to write a good answer two weeks after you've read the incoming letter for the first time.

If it takes too long to get the necessary information, try to speed up the process. If there are obstacles in the way over which you have no control, complain to someone who *has* control. In any case, do something. Don't let your letters just sit there. It's bad for your morale.

Should you apologize if your answer is late? I've answered this question before. If it's less than, say, ten days, I'd say no. There's no sense in drawing attention to the delay. But if it takes longer than that, then I definitely think you should apologize. Not only that, you should give your addressee a darn good explanation. Remember, he's already mad at you before he's even opened the envelope.

At any rate, as soon as you realize your answer will be delayed, send off some sort of interim letter to forewarn the addressee. Even a printed postcard is far better than nothing at all. For example, you might send him a card that says: "We're sorry but it will take us a week or so to get the information we need to answer your letter. Please bear with us in the meanwhile. Thank you."

A more specific letter is of course much better. One such letter, written by a bank vice-president, ran as follows:

Dear George:

This is just a note in connection with your telephone call yesterday. As soon as we hung up I assigned the job of running down the various exceptions in the reconcilement of your account to a member of our staff.

Today I have reviewed what we have developed so far but I find that it will take us one or two days more to get all the facts together. My purpose in writing is just to let you know that we are working on the problem and that I will send you a full report as soon as possible.

Sincerely yours,

More and more often nowadays, people write to the president of a corporation or to their congressman or senator when they want quick action on their case. I'm skeptical about the value of this, because the president or senator invariably sends the letter down through channels and it finally lands on the desk of the person who was responsible in the first place. Then the answer travels all the way up again and back to the inquirer. The whole process may well take more time than it's worth. However, it *is* true that a letter to a top official or congressman will always get an answer.

Most companies give priority to such letters to the top brass, and so do Washington agencies to letters addressed to a congressman or senator. I remember when I worked for the Office of Price Administration during World War II, there was a bright-red folder on everyone's desk that said "Congressional Mail" and had to be answered immediately.

The usual practice is for the company president or the congressman to send a brief acknowledgment and then pass the letter on through channels. Eventually the real answer travels back to the customer or citizen in its roundabout way. If you have the job of preparing such material for the company president or the congressman, remember that you're really writing to the person who complained.

For instance, I once suggested a rewrite for a letter from the Social Security Administration to a congressman. (The letter was of course signed by the commissioner.) The original went over the whole case the congressman had asked about and, toward the end, said that nothing could be done. My suggested rewrite started like this:

> I am very sorry I can't give you better news for your constituent Mr. Forano: his claim has been reviewed once more, but our Bureau of Disability Insurance still finds that under the law he's not entitled to any benefits. . . .

At least, when Mr. Forano got his copy of the letter, he'd know right away the congressman tried his best and the commissioner was sorry that nothing could be done.

Principle No. 2. *Show you're interested.* I said earlier that you should always study your source carefully to get material for your letter. Here I'm saying the same thing, but for a different purpose. While you're looking for essential facts, keep your eyes also open for minor or even trivial things, simply to show you're interested.

A classic example is a letter that came to a bank from a customer who'd moved from New York City to Bermuda. I seem to remember he'd settled there for good and started a new career by opening a school for scuba diving. He wrote to the bank to make new arrangements about his account.

The bank's answer started as follows:

> Dear Mr. Staubach:
>   We thank you for your letter advising us of your change of address.

Now really! How stony and unfeeling can you get? Here's a fellow embarking on an interesting new venture and all the letter writer can think of is "Thank you for advising us of your change of address." If I had written that letter, I would at least have said something like "I noted your new address with envy. The best of luck to you in your interesting new career."

Here's a less personal example. Every year in the spring the bank's corporate customers would send their annual reports, and every year thank-you letters had to be written for the various vice-presidents' signatures. I've seen dozens of these letters and they all followed the same pattern: "Thank you for sending me your annual report, which I read with much interest . . ."

The phrase " which I read with much interest" shows clearly that the writer did *not* read the report, or at least that he read it with little or no interest. Interest has to be shown and proved.

A good letter of this type would refer specifically to individual items of the annual report. It would say: "The picture of the new wing you added to the plant looks beautiful. . . . I found the story of your successful sales campaign quite fascinating. . . . On page 9 I read about your line of new products. It's a challenging experiment. . . ." And so on.

One way to show you've read the customer's letter carefully is to quote something back to him. I remember an old lady who wrote to the bank from Paris about various minor matters. Somewhere in her letter she said, "I know I am not one of your big, valued customers, but . . ."

The bank's answer dealt with the lady's problems and then said: "Please don't feel that we don't value you as a customer. We do indeed. We are delighted to serve you and hope to do so for many years to come."

Principle No. 3. *Don't be too short.* I've said before that brevity isn't always a virtue. Of course, in strictly routine business letters, it's pointless to waste words. The ideal is a brief, memo-type note that says simply "Here's the copy of your invoice" or "Mr. Ling hasn't called on us, nor have we had any inquiries on his behalf."

But as soon as you deal with a letter that isn't just a routine message, you can't leave it at that. A very brief letter may be offensive simply because it's too short. It may strike the addressee as a brushoff, even though it may have all the information called for.

Let's go back here for a moment to the model of a face-to-face conversation. If someone comes to your office to see you and asks a question, you can't simply say "The answer is such-and-such" and show him the door. Brevity, in this case, means discourtesy. You have to produce a certain quantity of words, simply to fill the time people think a polite answer should take. Remember that a very brief letter of one, two or three sentences takes just a few seconds to read. If you tried to put even a short, five-minute interview or phone conversation on paper, you'd have a letter of two single-spaced typewritten pages.

So again, just as a matter of sheer courtesy, you have to learn how to produce words in quantity. If you can't think of anything else to say, repeat yourself. If that still doesn't give you a reasonably long letter, repeat yourself again, in different words.

Last summer, on our annual family trip to Nova Scotia, we were annoyed by the long and over-meticulous customs inspection at the Canadian border. (They must have looked for drugs, I suppose.) We wrote a letter to the Canadian Department of National Revenue, and in due course got a very pleasant answer. Since we hadn't complained at the time, there was really no "incident" for them to investigate, and all they could do was to repeat their apologies. But they acquitted themselves nobly, using up 213 words to say essentially the same thing over and over. Their letter was thoroughly satisfactory.

Principle No. 4. *If it's bad news, say you're sorry.* This should be a matter of course, but it isn't so by any means. Sympathy somehow gets lost or mislaid in the course of keeping up with a daily load of business correspondence.

Remind yourself of what you'd say in personal conversation. If someone told you of a death in his family, you'd express your condolences. If he told you he was in the hospital, you'd say you were sorry to hear that. If he's out of a job, you'd sympathize with his plight. Do the same thing, as a matter of course, in your letters.

Yes, I know this often comes up in collection letters. A customer is behind in his installments and writes in to say he's lost his job or is seriously ill. Try to forget about the money for a moment. First of all tell him you're sorry for him. In the long run, you'll probably extend the payments anyway, so why not show him you're human?

You should express regret even when there aren't any of these major misfortunes. You should write "I'm sorry" or "We regret" whenever there's even the slightest thing that may strike the reader as unpleasant. If you notify him of a price rise, say you're sorry. If you can't answer his inquiry, say "We regret we can't give you the answer." If you need more information from him, say "We're sorry but we need more information before we can act on your application."

And so on. Express your regrets freely and invariably. After all, you say "Excuse me" whenever you brush past someone in an elevator or clear your throat while you're talking, so why not *write* that you're sorry about every little thing? It doesn't cost anything, and just shows you observe the conventional courtesies.

Some people object to this and say corporations aren't *really* sorry when they announce a price rise, and government agencies aren't *really* sorry when they tell an applicant that under the law he isn't entitled to anything. I don't agree with that attitude. Corporations *should* feel sorry for their customers if prices go up; after all, they're supposedly raising their prices not to make a bigger profit, but to keep up with rising costs. So why not tell the customer you regret this upward trend?

As to the applicant who's turned down because his situation isn't covered by the law, again, why not tell him you're sorry for him? This doesn't mean your government agency disapproves of the law as it was written by Congress; it simply means you sympathize with a human being who is in straits. Even the man whose claim has no leg to stand on may get a little comfort from the words "I understand how you feel." It's one of the most effective sentences in the English language.

This brings up the old problem of how to phrase a refusal, and particularly how to start it. Every textbook on business-letter writing has a little section on it. Usually they go into quite some detail explaining when you should say no right away and when you should lead up to it gradually.

I think the refusal should always come first. Nothing is gained by leading up to it in subtle ways, letting the reader wait for two or three minutes until he gets the bad news. He'll feel even worse if you've raised his expectation and then let him down.

Don't hem and haw. Start with your open refusal, and immediately follow it up with a clear and convincing explanation of the reasons why you can't give the addressee what he wants. After all, if you conduct your affairs in a businesslike fashion, you must have good reasons for saying no to a request. If it's particularly painful for you to say no, you can always say "We're extremely sorry" or "It is painful for me to say no to your request." (The best way to deal with an embarrassing situation is simply to admit your embarrassment.) But don't—repeat, don't—let the reader wait for your decision.

Principle No. 5. *If it's good news, say you're glad.* Of course it's easier to say yes than to say no. So I don't expect you to be too reluctant to start your letters with "We're glad to give you the information you want" or "We're happy to tell you your application was approved." Again, this is just a matter of normal everyday courtesy. Clerks behind counters smile at their customers—or at least are supposed to—and well-trained telephone operators say they're glad to help you in a pleasant tone of voice. Do the same in writing. Never mind that you don't feel like it on this particular gray morning. Train yourself. Develop a pleasant tone for your letters and stick to it.

I don't mean the bland, studiously polite tone used by many large corporations ("I hope this will alleviate your concern"), I mean something several degrees warmer ("Please don't worry"). You can do it. Exert yourself a little. Unbend. Smile on paper.

Principle No. 6. *Give everyone the benefit of doubt.* As I said before, in our system of law everyone is considered innocent as long as he's not proven guilty. Stick to this rule in your letters. Don't express your doubts and suspicions between the lines. Don't let the addressee feel you don't trust him. As far as you're concerned, he's honest. Forgetful, yes. A little sloppy maybe, yes. But not guilty of negligence. And certainly not deliberately dishonest. Don't accuse him, directly or indirectly. People resent it.

There's more of this in business letters than you might think. For example, a bank refunds a customer twenty dollars for a traveler's check he's reported lost. Later the check is cashed. Out goes a letter that says "In the event you believe the counter-signature is genuine, we would appreciate receiving your remittance of $20."

What does that mean? To my mind it means "We think you've cashed in twice on this check and you'd better refund us our money, or else."

I asked my banker students what they thought of this letter and they agreed the traveler was probably quite innocent. It's easy, and thoroughly human, to cash a check late at night in a bar in Rome or Stockholm and then forget all about it. Happens every day. Why write a letter with such a nasty undertone? The classic formula is "Probably due to an oversight . . ." and an excellent formula it is. Observe the rules of polite conversation.

Another instance is the stockholder who writes in that his quarterly dividend check hasn't arrived. He gets a replacement check and later gets the original check, which was somehow delayed. Since it's only a small check—say, $12.69—he doesn't pay too much attention, or maybe thinks this was the check for the next quarter. Anyway, he cashes both the original and the replacement check. In due course he gets a letter from the bank: "Apparently both these checks covering the same dividend were negotiated by you and we look to you for reimbursement for one of the checks and would appreciate your check or money order to cover same."

Why be so unpleasant? Why imply that the poor confused stockholder has committed a fraud? Again, it's far, far better to be pleasant. "We think you may have overlooked . . ." "It may have escaped your notice . . ." See what I mean? Give everyone the benefit of doubt. Don't be paranoid and suspect everyone of evil motives.

Principle No. 7. *Never send off an angry letter*. My father had an excellent rule. Whenever he felt like writing an angry letter, he dictated it right away, letting off steam, and then left the letter unsigned until the next morning. Next morning he looked at it again and tore it up.

Moral: Don't send off an angry letter. Not only that, don't send off a sarcastic letter, a mildly aggressive letter, an impatient letter— any kind of letter that may be considered offensive by the recipient.

Tone it down. Stick to a neutral, objective tone. Newspapermen have the excellent professional rule that they don't editorialize in their reports. Do the same thing in your letters. Don't intrude your opinions and emotions—except of course pleasure or sympathy.

Yes, you say, but how do you answer a letter that *deserves* a sharp answer? How about answering abuse? My advice is to ignore it. Throw it in the wastebasket and forget it. The sooner it drops out of your mind, the better.

Having been trained as a lawyer, I always used to be businesslike and answer every single letter I got. I was cured of that habit after I wrote *Why Johnny Can't Read*, a highly controversial book that brought me plenty of nasty, abusive mail. The only thing to do, I learned, was to throw all these letters away. Don't let them poison your system.

Sometimes a letter comes in that says "Don't answer this letter." Don't feel you have to disregard the writer's wish. Seize the opportunity. Don't answer.

Principle No. 8. *Watch out for cranks.* What I just said does *not* apply to crank letters. If you ignore them, you'll regret it. Answer them carefully and treat each crank with enormous respect.

During the time I practiced law in Vienna, there was a notorious crank by the name of Dr. Nahum Kreska. (That wasn't his real name, of course.) He was a disbarred lawyer who spent his life with innumerable lawsuits against anybody and everybody. Since Austrian lawyers are alphabetically assigned to give legal aid, Kreska could afford to run each of his lawsuits up to the Supreme Court and then, most likely, sue his legal-aid lawyer for damages because he'd neglected his duties. He was a familiar figure in the Hall of Justice, with his dark suit, bowler hat and rolled-up umbrella, and terrorized the entire legal profession.

Not long ago Mr. Robert Metz wrote a column in the *New York Times,* quoting complaint letters about brokers he got from small investors. "It is entirely possible," Mr. Metz wrote, "that some of those who complain are cranks, but it is also possible that they became cranky because of the kind of impersonal treatment we human beings dish out to each other in this mad, mad world."

One letter Mr. Metz quoted read: "My wife called Mr. Frost [the broker's customer's man] and told him she wanted to put in a buy order . . . Admittedly the order was small, 200 shares of a low-priced stock. Mr. Frost most ungraciously told my wife that the order was too small to even bother with and hinted strongly that he did not wish to be bothered by phone calls from investors with puny orders."

Cranky? Yes, perhaps. But the broker would have been much wiser to treat this customer with kid gloves rather than drive him into writing letters to the *New York Times.*

Principle No. 9. *Appreciate humor.* A surprising number of people inject a little humor into their letters, or at least are gracious and good-humored about their complaints. Don't give them the cold-shower treatment. Few things are so embarrassing as making a joke and having it greeted with blank, stony-faced silence.

If someone writes a humorous letter, show him that it made you laugh. If he went out of his way to be nice, tell him you appreciated the gesture.

Some years ago a man wrote a short letter to a Social Security payment center that said "Sir, would be pleased to receive my fishing license."

The payment center, never moving a muscle, wrote back that he should apply to the State Conservation Commission. It didn't occur to them that the man probably referred jokingly to his first retirement pay check. Surely someone with a little more imagination could have written: "Your first check will come through in about three weeks. Here's hoping you'll catch a big one on your first day out."

Principle No. 10. *Be careful with form letters.*

Of course, the ideal would be to use no form letters at all. But we don't live in an ideal world. Routine letters come in by the hundreds or thousands and there's no point in dictating a separate letter each time. So a form letter is prepared, and another, and another, and pretty soon a mass of form letters has sprung up, covering every conceivable situation.

The danger is that you're apt to get form-letter-happy. It's so much easier to send off a form letter and so much quicker, you say to yourself, giving yourself a nice alibi for being lazy. Well, resist the temptation. If the incoming letter is the least bit out of the ordinary, *don't* use a form letter. After all, *any* form letter is an indignity. Someone writes in about his unique personal troubles and what he gets back is a piece of paper, suitable for a thousand people in entirely different circumstances. Or at least, that's the way it feels to *him.*

So go easy on form letters. Use them only if you must—or if the case you're dealing with is indistinguishable from any other.

Even so, there are a few things you can do to take the curse off your routine response. First of all, look at the form letter. Can it be improved? (Of course, if you're a form-letter writer yourself, then it's your job to rewrite it, following the principles laid out here.) If you're using a form letter written by someone else, try to have it changed.

For instance, the Social Security Administration has a form letter for answering inquiries from people who didn't get their monthly check. It starts like this: "In reference to your recent communication(s) regarding benefit check(s), please note the paragraph(s) below indicated by 'X.' " This is followed by seven paragraphs with boxes for checkmarks. Why not start with "We're sorry you didn't get your check"? No reason—except the bureaucratic frame of mind.

Second, try to add *something* to the form letter to make it more personal. While you're inserting the address, checkmarks and other typewritten inserts, use the opportunity to add some other personal touch. Underline a suitable phrase, or add "Sorry for the delay" or "Please bear with us" or whatever else may fit. As I said, try to take the curse off.

Third, forestall further correspondence. Often the form letter has an empty space for inserting a specific part of your answer. Make sure it answers all the questions the inquirer has or might have.

Not long ago I got a letter from a credit card company—another one of those choose-from-our-menu letters with a number of boxed paragraphs to pick from. Enclosed was a Xerox copy of a charge for an item they'd mistakenly charged to someone else and were now charging to me. The letter was quite clear—except for the fact that the Xerox copy was so smudged and indistinct I couldn't make out the name of the store. If the writer of the letter had paid a little attention he'd have told me what store it was.

Fourth and finally, don't use a form letter for hedging. Hedging, as I said, means buck-passing and responsibility-dodging. The ultimate in hedging is when you pretend you haven't even heard the question. Someone writes in and drops a problem in your lap. The easiest way to get out from under is to simply ignore the problem.

In a recent article in the *New York Times,* an anti-war protester told how he refused to pay 23 percent of his 1968 income tax. He wrote the Internal Revenue Service that his conscience was in revolt against "the cruel injustices and bloodshed to poor and distant strangers being done under my flag, in my name, with my money."

Back came a form letter: "Dear Taxpayer: We are looking into the matter you brought up and should have the answer to you shortly. . . ."

Finally the answer came: The Revenue Service seized his bank account.

9 *Explain!*

In the fall of 1971 American Motors started a new advertising campaign, based on a simplified guarantee. It read:

> When you buy a new 1972 car from an American Motors dealer, American Motors Corporation guarantees to you that, except for tires, it will pay for the repair or replacement of any part it supplies that is defective in material or workmanship.
>
> This guarantee is good for 12 months from the date the car is first used or 12,000 miles, whichever comes first. All we require is that the car be properly maintained and cared for under normal use and service in the 50 United States or Canada and that guaranteed repairs and replacements be made by an American Motors dealer.

The campaign included TV commercials, in which the guarantee was simplified further. An actor playing an American Motors dealer said:

> Here's our guarantee. When you buy a new '72 from us, American Motors guarantees that except for tires we'll pay for the parts and the labor to fix anything that goes wrong that's our fault. Anything. We'll do this for 12 months or 12,000 miles at

no cost to you. All you have to do is take reasonable care of the car, use it under normal conditions, and get it fixed by one of us dealers. And that's it.

As you can see, the simplified guarantee wasn't simple enough for the TV audience. "Repair or replacement of any part . . . that is defective in material or workmanship" was translated to "we'll pay for the parts and the labor to fix anything that goes wrong that's our fault." The word "anything" was repeated to make it still clearer. The phrase "whichever comes first" was left out (too difficult to grasp). "All we require" was changed to "All you have to do." "Properly maintained and cared for" became "take reasonable care." And "guaranteed repairs and replacements" came out as "get it fixed."

Why were these changes made? Obviously because the writer of the TV commercial insisted the simplified guarantee had to be explained. He knew. He knew that words like "defective in material and workmanship" or "properly maintained and cared for" are too hard for average Americans to understand.

Explanation is an art—a difficult art. I've spent thirty years practicing it and know that it takes some doing to explain a legal concept like a guarantee to millions of people. But the art can be learned. It *must* be learned by anyone who does any business or professional writing. You never know when you'll come up against a problem of explaining to a layman some of the sophisticated machinery of modern life—guarantees, regulations, taxes, insurance and pension plans, and so on. They can and must be explained to laymen and there's a way to do it right.

Again, I've drawn up some ground rules—or points to remember—which I'll discuss one by one. Here they are:

The Eight Points to Remember

1. Nothing is self-explanatory.
2. Translate technical terms.

3. Go step by step.
4. Don't say too little.
5. Don't say too much.
6. Illustrate!
7. Answer expected questions.
8. Warn against common mistakes.

Let's begin with Point 1: *Nothing is self-explanatory.*

What I mean here is this: Don't give in to the temptation of giving your reader some ready-made explanation that'll do the job for you. That's the lazy man's solution. If you're called upon to explain something to someone who needs to understand it, don't hand him a pamphlet and say "Read it yourself."

I've battled against the insidious word *self-explanatory* in all my classes. My students know that for me it's the Number Two "bad word"—right behind the Number One "bad word," *inconvenience.* "Don't say 'Enclosed is our illustrated brochure which we trust will be self-explanatory'!" I tell them. "That's not good enough. Don't explain things by reference to another piece of paper. Don't try to do your job by proxy."

People by now are thoroughly used to finding extra pieces of paper stuffed in envelopes. Department store bills come with all sorts of enclosures—one piece of paper selling stationery, a second perfume, a third stockings. When I go through my mail, I automatically throw all that junk in the wastebasket. So, I'm sure, do millions of other Americans. Do you expect them to behave differently when they get a letter with a "self-explanatory" brochure? They won't. Your brochure will land in the wastebasket within a split second after they've opened the envelope.

Aside from that pull of the wastebasket, there's also the basic fact that nothing explains itself. No textbook teaches by itself. No map guides by itself. No printed piece of paper does the job it's supposed to do all by itself. There has to be a will and an eagerness to learn which, among the adult population, is normally absent. The common denominator of adults is resistance to education. They won't learn or study anything unless you give them a very good reason. Enclosing a "self-explanatory" brochure isn't one of them.

What you have to do is catch them while they're reading your letter. Explain what you want to explain right then and there. But, you say, should you just forget about your colorful brochure, which was done by professionals for a lot of money? No. By all means, enclose your brochure. But then refer to it in your letter specifically. Say "At the top of page 3 you'll find a detailed explanation of how to reconcile your account. Be sure to read it carefully and *keep it for future reference.* If you spend a few minutes now in learning how to do this every month, you'll save yourself a lot of grief." Or you might go further and repeat the information in your letter: "Remember the basic steps: . . ."

Anyway, don't rely on a printed source to do your job for you. Buttonhole your reader while he's reading what you wrote. He needs your explanation right now. Don't let him get away.

Point 2. *Translate technical terms.* When I worked for the Social Security Administration, I came upon the word *coinsurance* in their official "Medicare Handbook." The editor had carefully weeded out all technical terms from the handbook, but somehow *coinsurance* had escaped him.

What does the word *coinsurance* mean to you? Probably nothing—or, vaguely, some kind of insurance together with someone else. (My desk dictionary says "insurance jointly with another or others.") Well, you'll be surprised to hear that among social security experts *coinsurance* means something entirely different. It means that a Medicare patient is reimbursed for only 80 percent of what he pays his doctor and has to pay the remaining 20 percent himself. (He also pays some of the costs of a prolonged hospital stay.)

Technical terms are a sort of shorthand used among experts. There'd be no point for the social security people to say "the 20 percent paid by the patient himself" every time they want to refer to "coinsurance" *among themselves.* But since technical terms are so handy, there's a danger of forgetting how strange they sound to ordinary people. Words bandied about every day become as familiar as *bread* and *cheese.*

So watch out for technical terms. Look twice at every word you use to make sure it won't be unfamiliar to your reader. If there's a possibility that it will be, replace it by a clear translation or explanation. If this takes longer than your nice, quick technical term—well, that's too bad. Explanation *always* takes longer. A layman is someone who needs time to understand.

Point 3. *Go step by step.* This is particularly important if you're called upon to give someone directions. Everybody knows about the proverbial directions that come with unassembled Christmas toys and gadgets. I remember many, many Christmas Eves I spent sweating over jumbled, unintelligible directions to put together this, that or the other. One occasion I'll never forget was when we gave two of the girls new bicycles. They came unassembled and the directions were absolutely fiendish. It was 3 A.M. before we could even think of filling stockings.

Whenever you have to give directions to someone, first analyze the job from the point of view of someone totally ignorant who's confronted by it for the first time. Break it down into the smallest possible steps. Then describe each step carefully. Watch out for pitfalls. Be sure you're not talking about something your explainee hasn't come across yet. And for heaven's sake, beware of technical terms. Remember, there are millions of people in this world who don't know a sprocket from a dowel.

When I was working for the Social Security Administration, I was given the job of drafting new application blanks. The old ones had four pages crammed full with thirty, forty or fifty questions. By the time I was through, the number of questions on each blank had just about doubled. Following my own recipe, I'd broken down each question into its smallest possible units and rearranged them in a brand-new, step-by-step sequence.

Often you have to devise a different series of steps from those you'd follow yourself in going through the same process. For instance, the other day I invited a friend for dinner at my house. He'd never been to my house before and lived some thirty miles away, so I had to give him driving directions. Now if I had driven from his house to mine, I'd have chosen a certain route which is the quickest and most convenient. But I couldn't give that to him because he'd have had too much difficulty finding his way through a tricky maze of expressways. So I gave him a longer route which I knew he could follow easily.

Or, to take a simple example, yesterday I was at the supermarket. I bought a few groceries and some light bulbs. When I went through the check-out counter, I forgot to give the girl the light bulbs until after she'd rung up the groceries.

I expected her to ring up the light bulbs and add it all together. But she said, "Would you mind paying me first for the groceries? I'd rather do it that way."

So I handed her a ten-dollar bill and she gave me change for $4.28. Then she rang up the light bulbs, I gave her back the five-dollar bill she'd just handed me, and she made change again.

Moral: When you give directions, look at the job from the other person's point of view. What seems easy to you may be hard for them.

Point 4. *Don't say too little.* Always assume the other person is ignorant and doesn't understand things too well. Remember, the stupid citizen or customer has as much right to a good, clear explanation as someone with an IQ of 140. Spell it out for him. Don't be afraid of being too elementary.

A woman wrote to a social security office to ask how much she'd get as a widow's pension. The office answered: "The benefit of a widow age 62 or older is equal to 82½ percent of her deceased husband's primary insurance amount. Your husband's primary insurance amount is $177."

Do you think the poor widow whipped out a pencil and in no time at all came up with the answer? I doubt it. I rather think she tried to figure it out, gave it up after a while, and finally asked a schoolteacher or minister to help her. I hope somebody did tell her she'd get $146. But the district office certainly fell down on the job.

Point 5. *Don't say too much.* This is a much more common fault. The lazy letter writer has a natural bent for repeating the whole general rule regardless of whether the addressee is interested in it or not. Somewhere there's the specific answer to the inquirer's question, but he has to fish it out for himself.

Again, let's look at a social security case. A sixty-year-old widow asked whether she could get a widow's pension. She got the following answer:

> To qualify for widow's benefits the woman must meet the following requirements:
> a. She must be at least 62 years old;
> b. She must not have remarried;
> c. Her husband must have been fully insured at the time of his death;
> d. She must qualify as a widow under applicable State law or be entitled to a widow's share in her husband's intestate property;
> e. (1) The marriage must have existed at least 1 year before her husband died.
>   (2) If this provision cannot be met the widow:
>   a. At the time of her marriage, must have been entitled to a monthly social security benefit or could have been entitled except that she was not yet 62; or
>   b. She must be the mother of her husband's son or daughter.

As I said, the batting average of social security letter writers is pretty high. So this is possibly the worst letter they ever wrote. However, it makes a fine horrible example. What they should have written was, "We're sorry but you can't get a widow's pension until you're sixty-two."

Let this case be a lesson to you. Always study the incoming letter carefully and give the inquirer the answer to his question *but nothing else*. Don't try to think of remote contingencies. "Deal with the case before you," I tell my students. *"Don't try to answer the next letter. It'll probably never come."* (It's possible, of course, that the widow married her late husband just a few months before he died; but chances are she was married more than a year.)

Point 6. *Illustrate!* The way to explain a general rule is to show how it applies to a specific case. You have to illustrate everything you say. (And I don't mean pictures or cartoons; fancy artwork is another lazy man's excuse for not giving a clear explanation.)

Find an actual case that illustrates the principle. Find a large number of actual cases and pick the best ones to show exactly how the rule works in various typical situations.

One job I had to do for the Social Security Administration was to rewrite a general booklet describing various types of payments. I discovered that the agency had a thick file of local newspaper stories about individual cases of retirees, widows, orphans, wounded veterans, Medicare patients, babies, cripples, centenarians, and so on. I went through this whole file, which covered about five years, and carefully picked out all those cases that illustrated the basic principles of the system. Then I used the stories to clarify each point as I went along.

I don't know of any other way to explain a general system of rules. For each point you have to have one or two or three stories, the more dramatic and circumstantial the better. Indulge yourself in a little colorful writing. Tell what happened and what people felt and said. Don't be satisfied with the bare, abstract rules. Always have some anecdotes handy. Be a storyteller for once in your life.

Ideally, you should have three actual case stories to illustrate each range of situations. The first story would describe a typical case. For instance, to explain hospital insurance under Medicare, you'd tell about seventy-two-year-old Mr. Voltellini, who spent, say, three weeks in the hospital, ran up an average bill and had to pay nothing but the $68 deductible covering the first day. Two other cases might describe the upper and lower limits of this coverage. You may tell of sixty-six-year-old Mrs. Larkin, who stayed only one day in the hospital and, since her bill was under $68, had to pay for all of it. Then you'd take the case of eighty-three-year-old Mr. Braslov, who had to go back to the hospital after three months and had to pay the $68 a second time, since he was out of the hospital over sixty days. The three examples would give your reader the complete range of cases.

If you have no source of actual examples, you have to think some up. Be sure to give your reader typical cases he can compare with his own situation. I once worked with an editor who'd written up a fictitious example to illustrate an income tax rule. His "typical" taxpayer had a $100,000 salary. I asked him why he'd chosen such an affluent person. He said it made it easier to figure percentages.

Oh, yes, you should also give your fictitious persons names. Don't call them A, B and C, and don't call them Smith, Jones and Robinson either. What's wrong with ethnic names? Call them O'Leary, Rosenstein or Marchetti. Or, for that matter, give them Wasp names like Eliot or Thompson.

A few weeks ago I worked with a newly hired editor of a legal information service who'd written a brief article on holding a corporation board meeting over a conference telephone.

"Why would anyone do that?" I asked him.

"Well, imagine a small family corporation," he said. "The old man, the founder of the company, is ill in bed and can't attend the meeting. But he doesn't want to let go of things and likes to keep his finger in the pie. That's where a conference telephone setup would be the answer."

Now I understood. I told him of Galsworthy's *Forsyte Saga,* and of eighty-year-old Jolyon Forsyte, who'd long retired from business but enjoyed nothing so much as attending some of his favorite board meetings.

"Why don't you rewrite the article along these lines?" I said. "Start with a little story about the old man who wants to attend the meeting."

At our next training session the editor showed me his rewritten piece. This is how it started:

> John Forsyte, age 88, pushed his wheelchair closer to the window. The snow already completely covered three evergreens he had planted last spring. Almost 15 inches on the ground and more falling. What a day to have to travel 80 miles for a directors' meeting of the corporation he created, developed and still runs. But it's the important meeting at which a dividend is declared and the capital expenditures budget for the new year is authorized. He is determined to participate in the meeting.
>
> Mr. Forsyte can stay home and be present at the meeting . . .

"Splendid!" I said. "Was it very difficult for you to write this first paragraph?"

"Yes, it was," the editor answered. "This was the first time I ever did anything like that in my life. It was sort of fun, though."

Point 7. *Answer expected questions.* When you're through with your explanation to your reader or readers, you're *not* through. Just as every lecture or seminar should be followed by a question-and-answer period, so every explanatory letter or booklet should be followed by specific answers to questions likely to be raised.

The questions people usually ask are self-centered and immensely practical. They want to know, mainly, how much it's going to cost them and how long it will take. Perhaps also how much work it's going to be and whether it'll be unpleasant and painful.

Very often these are questions you haven't thought about in your presentation of the topic. Let me give you a few examples.

For instance, the makers of that unassembled Christmas bicycle should have answered, *at the beginning of their instructions,* the question that concerned me most: "How long is this going to take someone like me who's a complete, hopeless idiot about such things?" Don't laugh now. Instead, think about the importance of this highly practical question.

Or, to take an entirely different example, my doctor some time ago prescribed some medication I'd have to take over a long period. Being a good family doctor, he anticipated my question on how much these pills cost. Not only that, he gave me some good advice on how to get them cheaply.

My insurance agent was here a few months ago, discussing certain changes I wanted to make in my life insurance. He overwhelmed me with a ceaseless flow of figures about an alternative scheme, which he said was a poor idea to begin with. It took quite some persistence on my part to draw out of him the answer to my chief questions: "How much is my new premium going to be and when will the first check be due?"

Something went wrong with my car. I went to the garage I've been doing business with for many years. The owner gave me a long explanation about certain technical matters that were of no interest whatever to me. All I wanted to know was: "How much is this going to cost and how long will the car be laid up?"

Whatever you're dealing with, think of the average person, wholly uninterested in those lovely intricate details you're explaining to him—and probably incapable of understanding them anyway—but impatient to know the answer to his key questions: How much? How long? How disagreeable?

Of course, when you're writing for a large audience rather than one person, you're faced with the question of whose case you should discuss first. There'll be different types of people in your audience, and their circumstances will vary. To answer their expected questions, you should go strictly by numbers. Begin with the answers for 50 percent, then give the answer that fits 30 percent, next answer 10 percent, and then 5 percent, and so on. When you get down to very small numbers, stop. It's like your giving a lecture and answering questions from the audience afterward. At the very end of the session someone raises a hand in the back of the room and says: "My wife and I are separated but not divorced. Now my problem is this . . ." At which point you cut him off and say: "I'm sorry, sir, you've got a special problem I can't go into right now."

For example, in writing about those entitled to survivors' benefits under social security, you'd first write about the widow, then about the children, then about adopted children, stepchildren, illegitimate children, then about parents, then about a divorced wife (if the marriage lasted at least twenty years) and finally about a husband who'd been dependent on his wife's earnings. The most uncommon case has to wait longest for the answer to his question.

And the extremely unusual case—like the divorced dependent husband—wouldn't be mentioned in your general explanation at all. It would be a waste of space.

One more word: Some people seem to think that *everything* should be presented in question-and-answer form. I'm against this. In my experience this usually leads to strained artificial questions solely constructed to evoke a certain specific answer. Like this, for instance:

> Q. If I miss the last day for payment, is there a thirty-day grace period?
> A. Yes.
> Q. If I miss the grace period, do I have to apply for reinstatement?
> A. Yes.

Nonsense. This sort of exchange is as unrealistic as the family chit-chat on TV detergent commercials.

Point 8. *Warn against common mistakes.* No matter how well you explain things, some people will keep on making mistakes. They'll cling to their cherished bits of misinformation; they won't do what you told them a hundred times they should do; they'll disregard advice repeated incessantly and misunderstand what you spelled out in so many words.

Long-standing habits of error and inertia are extremely hard to overcome. In your explanations you must fight a ceaseless, active battle against these obstacles. Telling them isn't good enough. You have to repeat and emphasize what's right and point out strongly and loudly what's wrong.

A mild example I came up against in my bank classes was the business of filling out signature cards for opening an account. Bank people know from experience that customers often forget to put in their social security number, although there's a numbered box for it on the card. So to tell them, "Fill in your name, address, etc., and social security number" isn't enough. What the explanatory letter should say is, "Please don't forget to put in your social security number" or, better, *"Please don't forget to put in your social security number"* or, still better, *"Please don't forget to put in your social security number.* THIS IS VERY IMPORTANT."

If you want to remind your reader of something he's apt to forget or want to make sure he won't misunderstand you, use all the means at your disposal to get his attention. If you talked to him, you'd raise your voice and look him firmly in the eye until you're quite sure he's got the message. In writing, you have to do the best you can to get the same effect. Underline. Repeat. In extreme cases, use capital letters. (I don't like capital letters, but in an emergency, every handy weapon is worth using.)

The copywriters who prepare mail-order advertising letters have overused all these things so much they've lost practically all their effect. But that's only true for advertising letters. In an ordinary business letter or explanatory booklet these devices are still rare. Use them when you need them. Make sure your reader won't misunderstand or ignore you.

And, as I said, fight known, widespread errors. The Department of Health, Education and Welfare recently did a rather spectacular job of this kind. They put out a booklet called "Welfare Myths vs. Facts" to correct certain widespread wrong ideas. Welfare families, many people think, spend money on whiskey and big cars; most welfare children are illegitimate; the rolls are full of able-bodied loafers; people on welfare cheat, and most of them are black.

Wrong on all counts, the booklet says. Statistically, most welfare money is spent on food, clothing and shoes. Less than one-third of welfare children are illegitimate. *Less than 1 percent of those on the rolls are able-bodied unemployed males.* Fraud is suspected in less than four-tenths of 1 percent of all cases. And the largest racial group among them—49 percent—is white.

Will the booklet help correct people's wrong notions? Maybe not. But it certainly is a splendid example of the error-correcting technique of explanation. Think of it whenever you're faced by a job of explanation. The people you're writing for are bound to have some curious notions in their heads.

Root them out. Shed light into dark corners. Disabuse people of untruths.

10 *Report!*

The front page of the *Wall Street Journal* carries a daily column of brief reports on business, taxes and labor. Here's a typical example (October 5, 1971):

Doormen prove harder to recruit as the job gets riskier, loses prestige.

"I've been taking just anybody I can get," gripes the manager of Madison House, a Cincinnati high-rise. "You can always get some unemployed bum, but that's not what you want," adds a Chicago real estate man. The manager of Park Ten, a New York apartment house, attributes the shortage to psychological factors. "People don't like to say they're doormen."

Discouraging many prospective doormen is the crime problem. To make the job more appealing, some Chicago apartments pay a bonus for night work—$2.92 an hour versus $2.75 for days. Some New York doormen carry electronic devices that call police. Managers increasingly seek men with military records. "That's because they want people who have had experience handling small arms," says a San Francisco union official.

Rising unemployment boosts the caliber of applicants at some buildings: in Chicago an out-of-work lawyer recently worked six months as a doorman.

This is a model miniature example of a professionally written newspaper report. It begins with a brief, pithy summary of the findings; then follows the body of the report, consisting mainly of verbatim quotes from a variety of interviewees; and at the end there are some facts that don't fit the general pattern.

Business and government reports should follow this newspaper scheme, but usually don't. Instead, they ape the standard pattern of scientific reports: heavy, pompous language, loaded with technical terms; rigid avoidance of personal elements or live quotations; and a paragraph or two of conclusions at the end, rather than up on top. (Scientists, in fact, have learned to begin their reports with brief abstracts; but business doesn't seem to have heard about that.)

The more business reports I've seen, the more impatient I've become with their excessive formality and heavy-handedness. Why shouldn't the writer of a departmental progress report or branch audit write like a human being—that is, like a good, nosy newspaper reporter? Somehow the business reporter thinks he has to prove his seriousness and objectivity by following a cast-iron prescribed formula. He himself never appears; no one else is mentioned by name or, heaven forbid, quoted; and his most important findings are buried somewhere in the underbrush of the last page.

I think it's high time business reporters learn something from newspaper reporters. Their reports should have leads; they should learn how to quote from interviews; and they should keep their eyes open for the unexpected and contradictory.

The basic scheme of a good business or government report is—or should be—this:

THE THREE ESSENTIAL PARTS

1. Summary
2. Findings
3. Odds and Ends

If you're astonished at finding odds and ends among the three essential parts, that's exactly what I want you to be. I'll explain a little later.

First, let's look at Part 1, the *Summary.*

What distinguishes a report from a business letter is that it's meant to travel up the chain of command, in contrast to a letter, which goes out. The reporter is the person who has collected the data and knows most about what he's talking about. The next person to read it—his supervisor or department head—knows a little less and studies the report to add to his knowledge. The next person up the ladder knows still a little less—and reads the report with less attention and less intake of details. And so it goes—up and up—until the report lands on the desk of a top executive, who has only time to read the summary—and the notes and comments the report has accumulated on its way. In the end, therefore, the report is meant for someone who's totally ignorant of the specific situation and has to be taught. All he has time to take in is the gist. So there has to be an opening lead, or a synopsis or summary on a cover page.

Most business reports aren't written that way. A bank employee was sent out to a certain suburban area to study the possibilities of opening a branch. His report began like this:

> The best location for a branch to serve the Elmsford area is Sutton Street, in the vicinity of Brookville Boulevard.
>
> A service area for the proposed site would be bounded by 107th Street on the east, Hillside Avenue on the north, Parsons Street on the west, and Pacific Avenue on the south. Elmsford is one of the older sections of Queens, consisting mainly of one- and two-family homes. There were 13,649 occupied houses in the suggested area at the end of 1969. Most of these buildings or 89.9 percent were built during 1939 and earlier. The average median value . . .

And so on. Slowly and circumstantially, the report covered the geography and population of the area, its retail businesses, other banks already there, traffic patterns, mass transportation and market potential. Finally, there was a paragraph at the end that said:

> If further studies indicate that a $10.9 million deposit potential could support a small branch, then one is recommended.

This is a cautious conclusion, based on the evidence gathered. I don't quarrel with that. What I quarrel with is the position of that summary at the tail end of the report. Scientific reports used to be written that way, and scientists developed the habit of first reading the last paragraph of each paper to find out what the researcher had discovered. Now they have abstracts at the beginning and don't have to flip pages any more. Why not do the same thing for executives?

Newspapers and magazines carry models of this technique every day. Here's one (*New York Times,* November 26, 1971):

> Women of Italian, Polish and Russian-Jewish origin have had fewer children than white women generally, according to a Census Bureau study released today.

Here's another (*New York Times,* December 1, 1971):

> Trauma, a medical category of casualties resulting from a wide variety of injuries, is the leading killer of American civilians aged 1 through 38 and is a public health problem of growing importance.

Here's a third (*Travel & Leisure* magazine, January 1972):

> Life style and the creative use of leisure can be more important than diet or exercise in preventing heart attack. This startling conclusion is now emerging from a mass of research accumulated by San Francisco cardiologist Dr. Meyer Friedman. . . .

Some months ago, the editor of a business information service brought the draft of an article into one of my training sessions. It dealt with a speech on future fringe benefits made by a union leader. The article began:

> Over the past two decades, fringe benefits have become an increasingly important part of the collective bargaining agreement. While wages during this period have gone up 128 percent, fringe benefits have increased 339 percent. This rapid growth stems from several factors: first by pooling risks, the employer can get his employee more benefit for dollars spent than the employee could purchase himself; second, a fringe benefit is easier to sell to the employee than an equivalent increase in gross wages; finally, the typical employer now feels that it's his responsibility to help his workers face and overcome serious economic setbacks.
>
> In a speech before the 25th Annual Conference on Employee Benefits . . .

"Don't start in this slow, textbooky fashion," I said to the editor. "You don't need all this stage-setting and backgrounding. The subscribers won't stand for it. Start with a bang. Let's go over the rest of the article. What did the man say that was news?"

After some searching, we agreed that some of the labor leader's predictions were quite startling and even sensational.

"All right, put that on top," I said. "Rewrite the piece and let's go over it again next time."

A week later, he produced the rewritten article. Now it started like this:

> By the end of the 1970s you may be signing collective bargaining agreements granting employees such novel benefits as day-care centers for their children, free auto-liability insurance and complete medical care. This, in essence, is what was told to those assembled at the 25th Annual Conference on Employee Benefits.

"Fine," I said. "That'll make them sit up and notice."

Let's go on to Part 2—*Findings.*

The point here is that to a newspaperman, a report consists of facts gathered from interviews. (You can see this very clearly if you look closely at the *Wall Street Journal* report on doormen.) Even if he covers a government release or a prepared speech by a scientist, he'll try to get some direct quotes from the press conference or an added interview. From his point of view, information should always be oral—out of the horse's mouth.

For example, look at the following (*New York Post,* November 17, 1971). It's practically all verbatim quotes:

> If Mrs. Marx had stopped at two, Chico and Harpo would have had to make do without Groucho.
>
> But the two-child family, long the goal of zero population advocates, seems to be the coming trend. . . .
>
> At least half those interviewed cited "the environment" . . . Other women expressed little concern with the problem of over-population. . . .
>
> "I'd really like to go back to work someday," was a typical response. "Hell, I'd just like to to be able to get a good night's sleep. And you can't do that if you keep having babies. . . ."
>
> Lauri Vena, 24, . . . believes that "the planet can't afford" unlimited population expansion.
>
> "I used to want six," she said, "but now if I'm walking down the street and see a big family, I can't help but be disapproving. Or if someone tells me she's pregnant with her third child, I honestly can't congratulate her. I think kids are great, but if I wanted more than two, I'd adopt. . . ."
>
> One woman who plans to have more than two is Cheryl Vladeck, 24, the mother of year-old twins, a boy and a girl.
>
> "I loved being pregnant and loved giving birth," she said. "I don't believe in having 10 children or anything like that, but I do want to get pregnant again. Just because I had twins the first time doesn't mean I should be cast aside." (Another mother

of twins had the opposite reaction: "It was like nature was telling me something. I had a boy and a girl, the perfect family. I stopped right there.") . . .

A report (*New York Times,* September 17, 1971) on the impact of a new brokerage surcharge on small investors winds up like this:

> . . . One professional comments that he doesn't think the average round-lot trader cares much that it costs him $46.50 to buy 100 shares of a $25 stock. "He's either buying a stock like A.T.&T. for investment or he's a young doctor or lawyer who is buying crummy stocks he hopes will help him double his money," the pro says.
>
> "The A.T.&T. customer is actually buying a broker who knows the names of his kids and never forgets to ask about them."

You see? Newspaper reports are shot through with verbatim quotes—slangy, ungrammatical, irrational, but always enlightening. That last quotation tells more about the stock market than dozens of heavy, expensive books.

Why not use the same technique in your business reports? Suppose you've done a progress report on a certain project and have written the following sentence:

> According to preliminary estimates, it is anticipated that certain minor technical problems will be eliminated within a maximum of fourteen days.

Let's try a radical change. Write it like this:

> "We've got it licked," says project supervisor Nick Romano. "There are still a few bugs, but we'll get them all out in a couple of weeks. Take my word for it."

This is not only more interesting to read and better written, it also has more exact information.

Let's try another one. In a report on a branch audit you've written:

The records revealed a substantial decrease in deposits by Bizuchi Plastics Inc., which management ascribes to the impact of the 10 percent surcharge on imports.

Rewritten newspaper style, this reads:

"We've had a sharp drop in deposits from Bizuchi Plastics," says branch manager Art Ramirez. "They say the import surcharge has cut their sales in half."

Here again, we're up against something that'll come hard. You're not used to writing dialogue or direct quotes from what people said. Most likely, if you follow my advice and try it, it'll be the first time in your life.

But it's worth trying. More than that, it's indispensable if you want to improve your writing. Whenever you're preparing a report, collect your data with a pencil and a notebook. Write down what people *said*. You don't have to embarrass them by playing reporter; you can jot down their remarks afterwards. Just be sure to get it all down exactly as they said it. Most likely, they didn't express themselves in formal, carefully manicured English. They used slang, or perhaps even profanity. Try to get the flavor. Put it down the way it came out of their mouths, and you'll add enormously to the force and clarity of your report. Somehow, with the right quotes in the right places, everything will sound more convincing.

Practice being an interviewer. It's part of writing—in fact, it's a very major part of writing. I used to write my first few books on the basis of statistics and library research. Then I wrote my book *Why Johnny Can't Read* and, on a memorable day, I had to go out to Chicago to interview people and visit classrooms. It was something I'd never done before, and I found it vastly more interesting than tame library research. I think my excitement over what I found out got across to my readers.

Earlier, I quoted a bank report on a possible branch site. Somewhere in the text it said: "It has been rumored for quite some time that St. Thomas' Hospital will be demolished and the area which it now occupies will be used for new apartment buildings or a shopping center. However, to date no action towards this end has been taken."

How much better it would have been if the reporter had said: "Mike Gallagher, the all-knowing owner of the Four Corners Grill, gives St. Thomas' Hospital three more years at the utmost. 'Bound to come down,' he says. 'Those big contractors have it in the bag. Some say it's going to be a shopping center, some say a high-rise. Wanna bet?' "

Play with it. It may feel awkward the first time, but after a while you'll find it's fun. Fill your reports with people and let them talk.

Finally, Essential Part 3: *Odds and Ends.*

I promised you an explanation of this seeming paradox. Here it is.

Most reports are based on some kind of numerical or statistical survey. To describe statistical findings, you must give your reader two basic data: the average and the range. In other words, suppose you have a mass of statistics. There'll be what the statisticians call a normal, bell-shaped curve, with a big hump in the middle where the average cases are bunched, and two thin, petering-out tails at either end. At the extremes, there'll be cases that don't follow the general pattern at all.

Most often what you're after will be the typical pattern, the mass of cases. But equally interesting will be the "odds and ends"—the cases that stand out as unusual or are extreme in some way. If you're interested in progress, in doing something different, you'll keep an eye out for them. When Dr. Fleming first noticed the unusual mold that led him to the discovery of penicillin, he said, "My, that's a funny thing."

It's a fact of life that the seemingly marginal odds and ends you find *are* essential. Put them in your report and play them up. The unexpected little thing may be the payoff.

Newspaper reporters have a sixth sense for this sort of thing. Not long ago, the *New York Times* reported on a new study of high blood pressure. The study group urged a new community approach to diagnosis and treatment, particularly among poor black patients. Their report was quite lengthy, but the *Times* reporter went out of her way to interview some of the participating doctors on other aspects of the study. One of them, Dr. William B. Kannel, said: "An ideal blood pressure would be the lowest pressure you could achieve without going into shock. People with low blood pressure may complain that they're tired all the time, but they live for 120 years."

Another doctor, Dr. Ray W. Gifford, Jr., talked about the problem of getting patients who otherwise feel fine to take medicine day in and day out, probably for the rest of their lives. "Since all drugs have some side effects," he said, "treatment is not going to make the patient feel better, and it may make him feel worse."

These two offhand comments, to my mind, said more about the complexity of the problem than all the rest of the article.

Aside from the general findings of your survey or study, you'll always have some left-over, unclassifiable data. A survey of company dress policies by a business information service made a virtue out of this. At the end of the long survey, and after all the neatly classified findings, they ran a long list of "typical examples of disciplinary cases—and how they were resolved." For example:

Female secretary, 22: Wore micro-mini skirts; salesmen were spending too much time talking with her. Supervisor explained the situation to her; she complied. (Sales office, retail chain, Atlanta, Ga.; no set policy, individual standards.)

Male summer employee, 22: Wore long hair. Personnel manager called him in, asked him to have hair cut. Employee resigned. (Public utility, Pa.; no dress policy.)

Female clerical worker, 23: Wore very short skirt and insufficient underwear. Too revealing, since job involved bending into file cabinet. Was told to wear appropriate underwear and to work from kneeling position, to reach lower drawers of file discreetly. She took the hint. (Insurance firm, Ohio; has tacitly understood dress policy.)

Male management trainee, 24: Wore long, untrimmed shaggy

mustache. Personnel staffer suggested appropriate trim. He saw his barber. (Bank, Ohio; has dress policy, communicated through occasional staff mailers.)

Female typist, 21: Wore see-through blouse, no slip. Personnel officer discussed need for good grooming; employee asked to wear sweater over her blouse for the rest of the day. No repercussions. (Bank, Middle West; has stated dress policy, communicated to new employees via brochure.)

Male personnel assistant, 24: Wore hair too long; his boss, the personnel director, told him he would be fired if he didn't keep it trimmed. Employee complied; now complains his girl friend doesn't like his new "short" hair style. (Municipal gov't office, California; dress policy tacitly understood; nonconformists have been fired.)

Female clerk, customer service, 21: Wore skirts very short; reprimanded by supervisor and department manager. No repercussions, but employee did not comply. (Public utility, Far West; rules tacitly understood, but vary according to departments; general guides permit miniskirts 6 inches above knee.)

I wouldn't be surprised if many subscribers found these sample disciplinary cases more useful than the elaborate statistical survey.

In short, those odds and ends are often the real meat of your report. You never can tell. The reader of your report—the subscriber to the information service, or the executive vice-president—may be interested in aspects you don't know anything about. Perhaps he knows—in contrast to you—that the project manager goes on periodic alcoholic binges and wants to know how he behaved when you were there; perhaps he's grooming someone for promotion and is eager to learn how he performed; perhaps there's a new advertising campaign still under wraps which will depend on the findings of your report. Whatever it is, someone will look at those odds and ends you've collected with an interested eye. So you'd better look at them closely yourself too.

A classic example is a medical article I happen to have in my files.

It appeared in the *Journal of the American Medical Association* several years ago and dealt with the effect of five widely sold headache pills. Two of the pills were straight aspirin (one of them widely advertised); two were "extra-strength pain relievers"; and one was a buffered aspirin pill.

The main conclusions of the study were that (1) all five pills were equally good pain relievers; and (2) the buffered aspirin wasn't any better in preventing stomachaches than the straight aspirin pills.

But there was also a casual "comment" by the authors of the report: "The difference in the retail purchase price of the 5 drugs is not reflected in the effectiveness and comfort of the treatment, and the over-all performance of the less expensive agents in the group compares favorably with that of the more expensive ones."

In other words, the cheap, lesser-known straight aspirin pill was just as good as the four others, whose names were household words.

11 *Apologize!*

In the fall of 1966 my wife and I and our four younger daughters returned from a two-month-long, once-in-a-lifetime tour of Europe. We'd booked passage on the *Queen Mary* both ways and were now approaching New York.

Two days before our arrival, there came a message over the loudspeaker that passengers could order a rented car for pickup at the dock. The message was from a widely known car rental company I'll call Intercar. I realized with a shock that I'd no idea how to get my family plus a dozen pieces of luggage from New York to our suburban home, twenty miles to the north. So I quickly made the reservation.

Sure enough, when we landed in New York, there was a young lady from Intercar—bright and cheerful at 8 A.M. on a dismal October morning—who greeted us, checked our name on her list, and pointed out our waiting station wagon. We got in, drove home in forty-five minutes, and walked into our house.

Three years later we were in Europe again, this time for the wedding of our oldest daughter. When the time came for going home, I—being by now a wise and experienced world traveler—phoned the London office of Intercar and ordered a station wagon for pickup at the dock. (This time we traveled on the *Queen Elizabeth 2*.) The next day I got a confirmation which said "Station wagon to meet QE2 at New York dock on 24 Sep. 1969 at 8 a.m."

When we arrived in New York, I confidently walked to the Intercar desk, expecting to see the same cheerful blonde. But she wasn't there. Instead, there was a middle-aged man who looked decidedly grumpy.

Yes, he had my name on his list, together with nine others. He had a station wagon and said he'd drive us over to the mid-Manhattan Intercar office, where we'd get a car to go home.

"But don't you have a car here on the dock for us?" I asked incredulously.

He was unimpressed. They did it this way now, he said. "Just wait until your luggage is cleared through customs and then come back here. Oh, by the way, there are four people ahead of you."

I was furious, but there was nothing I could do. When we'd finally got our nine pieces of luggage through customs, we assembled with our sad little heap at the place where the man had been. He was nowhere to be seen. Eventually he turned up, but had to shuttle back and forth twice more to the Intercar office until he could take us on. By then a good hour had passed since we'd gotten through customs.

Finally he was ready for us. We squeezed into his station wagon and went to the Intercar office. There we unloaded and I talked to a girl behind a counter. She pulled out a card with our reservation—for a station wagon to be waiting for us at the dock!—and said we'd have to wait until they could find a car for us. I protested vigorously. She was wholly indifferent. I called for the man in charge of the office and explained the situation to him. He was bland and unhelpful.

After another hour they had a car for us. It was *not* a station wagon, but a large sedan. They said it was large enough for us. By some miracle, and through sheer desperation, the six of us with our nine pieces of luggage somehow got in. We drove off northward. Around noon, five hours after landing in New York, we got home.

Two days later I fired off a letter to Intercar. You can imagine that it was heated and highly circumstantial. I can't remember whether I said that Intercar had written off their transatlantic boat trade because it was no longer lucrative enough. At any rate, that was the obvious explanation for what had happened.

A month passed. Finally a letter arrived, dated October 22, 1969. Here it is:

Dear Mr. Flesch:

Your letter of September 26th concerns me and I extend apologies to you for your unsatisfactory experience at New York.

This kind of service obviously was inexcusable and, therefore, I will not even try to offer an explanation for the problems that contributed to your dissatisfaction. However, as a result of your having taken the time to write to me, we have the opportunity of taking corrective action. The management involved has been asked to investigate the conditions outlined in your letter so that other customers will not be subjected to the inconvenience and aggravation you experienced.

Mr. Flesch, we value your business and hope you will give us the opportunity of regaining your confidence on your next car rental.

Sincerely,
H. M. Glabkin
Administrative Assistant
Customer Relations Department

I think this was the worst answer to a complaint letter I ever saw. It did nothing to pacify me. In fact, even now, after two years, I'm looking back at the episode in sheer fury. (I hope my description has brought this out.) Mr. Glabkin (that was not his name), far from soothing me, made things worse. All those oily, ready-made phrases and not a word about what his company had done to me! They'd obviously accepted my reservation in London, knowing full well that the pickup service at the dock had been discontinued. They hadn't offered a word of apology or explanation on that dreary, interminable morning. They hadn't even bothered to give me a station wagon when they could have done so. And now they capped it all with that insufferable public-relations-prose letter, written four weeks afterward.

I tried to picture Mr. Glabkin. Obviously he wasn't a long-haired, hippie-style young man. No, no. He surely must be a clean-looking, square, neatly groomed young man, with a degree in business administration and well in line for promotion in the company. He could write letters like that by the dozen, and probably did.

Then I tried an experiment. I imagined I'd complained about an overflowing ashtray and had gotten Mr. Glabkin's masterpiece in return. Would it fit? I reread the letter very carefully *and found that it did.* (You can do the same experiment and check me.) What I'd gotten was the company's all-purpose answer to complaints.

Well, enough of that. I hope this horrible example impressed you. Answers to complaint letters are the final test in business-letter writing and in my courses I always treated them as such.

Each time toward the end of the course I'd assemble from the company or bank a bunch of complaint letters that had come in during the past few weeks. Then I'd pick one or two as the final test for my students. In this way, I've seen more complaint letters than most people and have come to certain conclusions on how to deal with them. Here are my four guideposts.

The Four Guideposts

1. Take the complaint seriously.
2. Explain what happened and why.
3. Don't shift the blame.
4. Don't just write—do something.

Let's look at these guideposts. First, *take the complaint seriously.*

The main trouble with the Intercar way of writing a letter of apology is that it sounds so phony. Far from taking my complaint seriously, they just gave it to Mr. Glabkin and after four weeks he sent me their standard letter. Not a word about what actually happened, no explanation, not even a decent apology. ("I extend apologies to you" just isn't good enough.) What *did* happen that morning? Was this just an isolated mishap or was it, as I suspected, a deliberate new policy? Were the people reprimanded who treated me so discourteously? Was something done to prevent a repetition? No answers. Obviously, Intercar treated me and my complaint *not* seriously. The unmistakable impression was that they didn't give a damn.

If *you* have to write such a letter, what can you do to make it sound sincere? It's not an easy question, and there are no quick answers to it. Certainly you'll have to stay away from those tired old phrases that sound so phony and indifferent. Don't say "Thank you for bringing this matter to our attention" or "We are grateful for the opportunity to explain." Clearly you don't mean that. *Nobody* is grateful for a complaint letter.

And don't say "I extend my apologies." At least say "we regret" or "we're sorry" and show that you mean it. "Disturbed" and "distressed" aren't good either. Try to write something you'd *say*. Perhaps "We're really unhappy about your letter, because unfortunately this is a situation that has plagued us for several weeks." Or: "I'm puzzled by your letter and unhappy about it, because we've never had a complaint of this type." Or: "Yes, you're quite right. This is something that should never have happened."

Which brings us to Guidepost No. 2. *Explain what happened and why.* You can't convince a complainant that you're taking his case seriously if you don't explain exactly how and why it all happened. Go into details. (Remember, the longer your letter, the more effective it'll be.) Show you're concerned; you've interviewed the people who were there; you're giving the whole problem serious attention.

Normally, when you're answering a complaint letter, you're writing on behalf of a large organization to an individual customer or citizen. This gives you the advantage of showing him how the problem looks from *your* side. For instance, say Miss Mary Kostka writes a letter to her bank complaining that she was twenty minutes late coming back to her office from lunch because she had to wait half an hour in line to cash a check. (It takes her twenty minutes on the subway each way to go from her office to her bank and back.)

Now if in your answer you explain truthfully and in detail the bank's problem in hiring enough tellers to give reasonably quick service during the lunch hour, then maybe Miss Kostka will be impressed. She'll begin to see the problem from the bank's side, realizing the number of tellers and the amount of added salaries it would take to make sure that she—and thousands like her—are served faster.

Usually an individual customer has no idea of the business problems that led to the specific situation he or she's complaining of. If you carefully explain your problems, they'll probably be flattered by the attention and by the glimpse behind the scenes of big business.

Sometimes the company or bank has a certain policy and the customer thinks it's wrong. In such a case the poor letter writer says "Let me explain that this is our policy" or words to that effect.

"Don't do that," I tell my students. "Don't say it's our policy. All this means is, We do this because we do this. The customer has complained because he says the policy is wrong. You have to explain to him either why we're sticking to it or that we've decided to change it."

For instance, let's say Mrs. Mildred Tolliver complains she's had to pay a one-dollar charge for a cashier's check under one hundred dollars, while the bank across the street doesn't charge a penny for such checks. There are only two ways of answering that sort of complaint. Either you write "Yes, we know, but we've analyzed our costs and simply can't give out these checks without charge" or you write "We're looking into it to see what can be done."

The simple point here is that you have to tell the truth. Subterfuges won't do. Explain what happened and why. Either it was a mistake and you'll correct it or it's a set policy and then it's your job to defend it. There must be a rational explanation. Tell them what it is. People will listen to reason.

Some years ago, my bank class grappled with a complaint letter from a woman who lived on New York's Upper West Side. I'll call her Miss Margaret Campbell. She complained that service during evening hours had been discontinued in all branches in her area. The fact was that the bank had ordered the closings because of the rising crime rate, but word from on high was that we were not supposed to say so in our answer.

I gave these instructions to my students, but the results were poor. There simply was no good way of answering that letter as long as the true reason was concealed. What the bank should have done was admit the situation openly. (This was some years ago; by now of course everyone knows about the problem.)

Another example: A customer—let's call him Mr. George Snyder —complained he'd been charged seventy-five cents for having deposited a check that was later returned because of insufficient funds. Mr. Snyder said this was unfair: why should he pay a seventy-five cent handling charge just because someone else had given him a check that was no good?

The answer to this was simple. Yes, the bank could well understand that the seventy-five-cent handling charge seemed unfair to Mr. Snyder, but the actual work cost the bank that amount, and there was no other way of recovering it. Mr. Snyder of course had a claim against the person who gave him the bad check and should add the seventy-five-cents extra charge to that claim. All other New York banks handled the problem the same way.

Next, Guidepost No. 3. *Don't shift the blame.* Quite often you get a letter with a complaint about something done by someone else in the company. Don't give in to the temptation to say so in your answer. There's no point in explaining to the irate customer that it wasn't your fault but that of the accounting department, or that Mr. So-and-so in the local branch office was to blame.

From the point of view of the aggrieved customer or citizen, the corporation or government agency is all one. He doesn't care about those interoffice struggles or jealousies. Never mind trying to shift the blame. It's still your company or agency that's done wrong, and giving someone the runaround just makes things worse.

Of course sometimes it *was* a specific person who was responsible.

Say a sales clerk in a department store was rude and the customer complains. If so, answer that the clerk was reprimanded for his behavior; perhaps add that you've reminded all clerks that they should never be rude. But again, put this in your answer only if it's the truth. Somehow, if you haven't actually followed up on the complaint, your letter will sound phony.

Let's say Mr. Paul Wang writes a letter to his bank that at 6 P.M. on a certain evening he found himself with only one subway token in his pocket and went to a branch office to cash a check. The guard at the door was just locking up. Mr. Wang explained his emergency to him, but the guard just laughed and said the bank was closed. Mr. Wang noted his badge number and went home to write his letter of complaint.

The only answer that'll satisfy Mr. Wang is that the guard was reprimanded and *all* guards were reminded of their duty to be courteous. And the only way to write such a letter with conviction is to actually do it.

Now we come to Guidepost No. 4: *Don't just write—do something.* This is the sticking point. I'll have to convince you that improving your answers to complaint letters may cost you money.

Let's not kid ourselves. If someone writes in who thinks he's been mistreated by your company, he probably won't be satisfied with just soothing words. Something more is needed to restore his good will toward your company, and the something more has to be a tangible token of your remorse. People don't write complaint letters unless they've really suffered some damage or their feelings have been wounded. Mere words usually aren't enough to calm them down.

On principle, every answer to a complaint letter should undo the damage that was done. Sometimes this is a matter of routine, as when a store replaces defective merchandise or a bank that has erroneously returned a check writes a letter to the creditor protecting its customer's credit standing.

But sometimes things are not so simple. Let's look at some of the cases just mentioned.

What, for instance, would you do about Mr. Snyder, who complained about the seventy-five-cent handling charge for someone else's bad check? As I've said before, there was a good business reason for this charge and Mr. Snyder was told why it was necessary. Will this make him change his mind about the unfairness of the whole thing? Probably not—it rankled so deeply that he wrote a long letter about seventy-five cents.

The thing to do is to waive the charge in his particular case and credit his account with seventy-five cents. You'll say this is inconsistent; you can't defend your policy and then turn around and make an exception for Mr. Snyder. But why not? Part of the secret of good writing is inconsistency. Why not bend a rule in a special case? It won't do any harm and it'll do the job of showing Mr. Snyder that the bank cares about his good opinion.

You have to realize that good public relations are a precious asset. As soon as someone complains—even if it's just seventy-five cents' worth of a seeming unfairness—you've suffered a small loss of this asset and it's worth money to recover it. If you work for a bank, waive such minor charges as a matter of routine. It doesn't matter whether the charge was justified or not. Once the damage was done and a customer's good opinion was lost, it pays to get it back. Never mind the bank's set policy; do what's necessary to repair the damage.

Let's apply this principle to some of our other cases. How about the one-dollar charge for the cashier's check under one hundred dollars? Again, let's explain the policy and then, inconsistently, waive the charge for Mrs. Tolliver. She'll tell her friends and neighbors about that nice bank—they don't do this for everybody but they did it for *her*.

Now you'll say that Mrs. Tolliver's friends and neighbors will descend on your bank and ask for cashier's checks under one hundred dollars free of charge. But you're wrong. Cashier's checks in small amounts aren't something everyone needs every day, and these dire consequences are remote. Don't worry about what might happen in rare contingencies. At the moment it's your job to make Mrs. Tolliver feel better about your bank. Do it. Spend the one dollar for the purpose.

Next, what can we do about Mr. Wang and his encounter with the rude guard? As I said, he'll probably be satisfied to know that the guard was chewed out. No extra expenses needed here.

Now we come to Miss Campbell, who's unhappy because her bank branch is no longer open evenings. Let's assume we gave her the true explanation and told her about the crime wave in her area. Is there anything else we can do for her? Well, we can tell her about mail deposits, explaining exactly how to do it and sending her the necessary forms. Not too helpful, but it's the best we can do.

Finally there's Miss Kostka, who lost so much time trying to cash a check during her lunch hour. Let's do something really nice for her: let's give her a card signed by the assistant branch manager so she can come in during the lunch hour and get preferential treatment. She'll go to the assistant manager and he'll slip behind the counter and cash her check for her.

Impossible, you say? Not at all. I had an assistant branch manager in one of my classes who worked in a posh neighborhood on Manhattan's Upper East Side. She told me she never let her mink-coated customers stand in line to cash a check. Rather, she'd let them sit down by her desk while she discreetly attended to their little chores.

Why not give poor Miss Kostka the same treatment? Again, you'll say she'll abuse the privilege and everybody will ask for the same treatment as soon as word gets around. But people aren't like that. I doubt whether Miss Kostka will use her special-preference card very often, except in a real emergency. And I don't think her friends will immediately clamor for the same kind of card. Don't worry. Obey your generous impulses. It'll do wonders for public relations.

And now, what about Mr. Glabkin and the letter he wrote for the Intercar company? I've often thought about what would have been a really good solution to the problem. Naturally, a properly written letter of apology should have had a complete, truthful explanation of the mistreatment I suffered and a really sincere, humble apology. But would that have been enough? The answer is no. Nothing would have changed my feelings about Intercar except a refund of the seventeen-dollar car rental I paid that day. It's the least they could have done.

This chapter has a happy ending. Let me tell you the tale of the chicken and the screwdriver.

Last spring we bought a package of frozen fried chicken at our supermarket. When we opened it, we found a nice little screwdriver.

I laughed and added the screwdriver to my collection, but my wife said I should write to the company. It was called, say, the Terence I. Meadows Company of Brookdale, Mass.

I wrote the following letter:

> Gentlemen:
>
> Yesterday we bought one of your frozen fried chickens at our local supermarket. Inside the package we found, along with the chicken, a screwdriver. This isn't exactly what one expects to get with chicken.
>
> I just thought I'd bring this incident to your attention.
>
> Sincerely yours,

Within a week I got an answer. It read:

> Dear Mr. Flesch:
>
> Stunned is the only word to describe the reaction amongst the personnel at T. I. Meadows, Inc., upon receipt of your letter dated April 21, 1971. We have never before experienced any product complaints featuring a piece of equipment or something of the like contained in one of our products. Quite obviously, a screwdriver should be large enough to have been seen by anybody packing the chicken, and it is incredible that such a thing could have occurred. We are at a complete loss as to how this might have happened, since production people are not permitted tools or the use of them in their jobs. We are most pleased that

you brought this incident to our attention and rest assured that we will follow through with action to see that what would appear to be impossible, cannot ever happen again.

Recently, there has come on the market a very sensitive magnetic apparatus which would enable us to detect any piece of metal, including something as small as a staple, in any of our products. We have issued the approximately $5,000.00 purchase order for one of these pieces of equipment to run all of our products through. Had this item been available earlier, we would have most certainly detected a piece of metal as large as a screwdriver.

We simply cannot offer any excuse as to how this happened and are only glad that neither you nor your family suffered any discomfort from this item being in the package. It is our desire to reimburse you for the cost of the item in order that you may be aware that we would like to have you try another package of our chicken, to see for yourself that it is wholesome and safe to eat. Therefore, I am enclosing a check to the sum of $1.75, in order that you may try another box of our chicken. Thanks, again, for your interest and cooperation in bringing this matter to our attention.

Sincerely yours,
Terence I. Meadows, Inc.
Joseph T. Hausmann
Dir. of Food Technology

I'm not saying that Mr. Hausmann's (not his name) letter follows ull the rules laid down in this book. But it's long and detailed and shines with genuine interest and sincerity, illustrating beautifully the four guideposts in this chapter. Mr. Hausmann, far from dismissing the little screwdriver with a shrug, took it extremely seriously, even telling me about their new five-thousand-dollar metal-spotting machine. He explained clearly their packing setup and why it seemed so inexplicable that the screwdriver got into the package. He certainly didn't try to shift the blame. And he went out of his way to send me $1.75 just to clear the good name of his company.

He succeeded beautifully. I showed his letter to my wife and daughters and we had a fine meal of frozen fried chicken the next day. Ever since, we've all been very fond of Terence I. Meadows, Inc.

12 *Keep It Up*

I don't know how many times I've walked into a classroom to start the last session of a seminar or training course. Over the years, the pattern of that last session has always been more or less the same. First I return the students' final test papers and go over them individually. Next I briefly review the course as a whole. And then I wind up with a few final words to the students, who'll now go back to their desks or jobs to apply what they've learned.

I'll try to do much the same thing in this last chapter. Of course you haven't written a final test paper, but you can do something of the same sort and try to grade yourself. Here's what I suggest.

After you've studied this book, take three or four of the more important letters you have to write and do them strictly by the rules I've given you. Make extra copies of them. Then compare your work with the following model examples:

1. The letter "Here's the invoice" on page 7.
2. The letter beginning "Mr. Ling hasn't called on us" on page 51.
3. The letter beginning "Yes, we were surprised" on page 98.
4. The "Dear George" letter on page 101.
5. Mr. Hausmann's letter on pages 149 and 150.

How do your letters stack up against these models? Be honest with yourself. Give yourself a grade. If you've really learned something from this book, it'll probably be a B or a C. (A's are always rare, you know.)

The value of a test is that it shows you where you're weak. Most likely, your letters are not as human as they should be, and not focusing clearly on the essential facts. (If you're a woman, you're probably better on the human touch; if you're a man, you're probably better on the facts and main points.) Work on these weaknesses. Go back to chapters of the book you've slighted. As long as there's room for improvement, try to do better.

All right. Now let's go quickly over the course once more. To begin with, there's the "talk on paper" technique. Train yourself relentlessly in using contractions. Put in apostrophes with a free hand. While you're at it, strike out *that*s and *which*es. Train your nervous system to tolerate prepositions at the end and repetitions of simple words. Learn to shrink away from "elegant variations"—synonyms used just to avoid repetition. Use questions with question marks. Learn to live without *above, hereafter, said* and *such.*

Next, become a better researcher. Use a pencil. Take notes. Write in the margin. Mark up your sources. Look for the stuff you'll use in your writing and make sure it doesn't get away from you.

Look for the facts beneath the facts—motives, hidden purposes, underlying reasons. Answer what was in the other person's mind, not what he expressed on paper.

Now we come to the organization of your letter or report. Train yourself *not* to start with "a piece of paper." Put all reference data in a caption and start with the main point. Your letter must have a lead. Spend some time formulating the lead before you start dictating. After a while, you'll learn to do this faster and finally it'll become automatic. But begin with a lead—always.

Next item: Sentence length. Remember, it's easy to split your sentences up so you get an average of twenty words, but harder to get below that figure. To write average sentences between fourteen and sixteen words, you have to learn to write *really* short sentences every so often. The way to do this is to do it. Rev up your mental engine and make it run a little faster. Then watch your letters and reports wake up from their customary torpor.

Next comes my list of sixty "bad" words. Naturally, you can't cut all of them out at once, but you can train yourself to do it gradually. Start with those that are direct synonyms of simpler words—like *prior to, subsequently, sufficient, terminate, in the event that.* Force yourself to avoid these words and replace them by *before, later, enough, end, if.*

After those simple substitutions, tackle such other words as *determine, facilitate, require.* Weed them out wherever they show up.

Finally, see whether you can write without *any* of the sixty words on my list—and some others you may be addicted to. (Everybody has his or her own pet pomposities. Suppress them. Banish them from your vocabulary.)

You'll find—to your surprise—that it's possible to live without those words. You'll learn to appreciate the joys of simple language.

Now we come to the human side. Write for *people.* Use the devices I showed you to make your letters as personal as possible. Express your natural feelings. If it's good news, say you're glad; if it's bad news, say you're sorry. Be as courteous and polite as you'd be if the addressee sat in front of you. (At least I *hope* you'd be polite.) Show him you're interested in his case. Act like a human being.

When you have to explain something, remember what Will Rogers said: "Everybody is ignorant, only on different subjects." You may know all there is to know about your specialty, with technical terms and handy abbreviations tripping off your tongue, but the other fellow needs a slow, painstaking explanation. Be patient. Define every term he might not know. Illustrate every step with simple or even home-spun examples. Repeat the process until you're reasonably sure you got through.

You may think I've slighted report writing in my book, because I gave it just one little chapter. But now that you've gotten this far, you'll know that I don't believe in special writing techniques for special purposes. Good writing is all one. Reports, just like letters, should have leads, they should be written in clear, simple English, and they should show you're human.

Reports are usually based on interviews. Learn to be a good interviewer. Put in quotes of what people said and *how* they said it.

The one thing special about report writing is what I called the odds and ends. A good reporter always looks out for the unexpected. After all, he's reporting on a survey, a piece of research or, anyway, a series of observations. If he's worth his salt, his report will turn up something he didn't expect to find. That unexpected something is what the reader of the report will be interested in. So be on the lookout for the marginal, even the trivial, the seemingly irrelevant—*and put it in*.

Finally, the letter of apology. Again, be specific, be human, try to understand and reply to what's at the root of the complaint. Don't let it go at that, but do something extra. Waive the charge, even if it's company policy *not* to waive it. Make an exception. Bend the rule. Go out of your way to make people feel better about your company or organization.

And that's it. I've run through the high spots. Oh, yes, I know this book doesn't cover certain specific types of writing you may be interested in. There's nothing here on how to write memos, or credit letters, or collection letters, or corporate minutes. I won't apologize for that. As I said before, I think the basic principles of this book apply to *all* types of writing. Do them in the spirit of this book, and you'll come up with crisper memos, more informative credit letters, collection letters that bring in more money faster, and corporate minutes that will stand up as evidence in court.

And now a final word. Don't put this book away after you've read it. Put it on your desk and keep on using it. Check up on yourself from time to time. Reread a chapter here or there, check on my lists of numbered reminders, go over the sixty-word blacklist again, and count the words in your sentences to see whether you're still in line.

I know from experience that everybody, even the most enthusiastic student of my books and courses, has a tendency to backslide. It's inevitable. Here you are, trying to write clean, simple, informal prose, and everybody around you writes pompous, bureaucratic gobbledygook. Your incoming basket is full of the stuff, and it takes a real effort to free yourself from this incessant, insidious influence on your mind and your writing.

I've said you should write the way people talk—at lunch or over the telephone. But more and more people do use this stiff, formal language in their ordinary, daily conversation. Yes, I've heard people use *prior to* and *indicate* freely and naturally as if they didn't know of any other words. I've heard policemen on TV refer to criminals as *perpetrators*. So you not only have to return to simple English, you have to actively stem the tide and defend your mind and language against assaults from all sides.

If you do it, you'll find there are rewards. When you write a particularly good lead or a crisp, elegant paragraph, or a letter that conveys your thoughts clearly and simply, you'll feel a glow of creative achievement. Treasure it. It's something you've earned.

There'll also be material rewards. As a matter of sheer observation, if you stick to my style of writing, you'll probably be promoted. This is the age of large organizations where it's easier to catch the eye of a superior by what you write than by what you say or do. Write the way I've tried to teach you and your stuff will stand out and be noticed. Everything else will follow.

What concerns me is that as you're climbing the ladder of success you'll get away from writing. Your time will be taken up more and more by administration, and you'll delegate the handling of words and sentences to subordinates. Please don't abandon writing altogether. Keep a little time open each day to attend to some correspondence. And keep a watchful eye on everybody else's writing.

When you get the opportunity, see to it that the letters that go out from your department are clear, effective and human. Try to get control of form letters, so they won't undo all the good work done by individual correspondents. And try to curb the lawyers so they won't mess up the decent prose written by someone else, until it's clogged up by interminable qualifications and protective clauses.

In other words, keep it up. In this age of general pollution, clear, simple language is just as important as clean air, land and water.

Do your bit. Say what you mean in plain English.

Index